The Theory of Culture-specific Total Quality Management

The Theory of Culture-specific Total Quality Management

Quality management in Chinese regions

Carlos Noronha

palgrave

First published 2002 by
PALGRAVE
Houndmills, Basingstoke, Hampshire RG21 6XS and
175 Fifth Avenue, New York, N.Y. 10010
Companies and representatives throughout the world

PALGRAVE is the new global academic imprint of
St. Martin's Press LLC Scholarly and Reference Division and
Palgrave Publishers Ltd (formerly Macmillan Press Ltd).

ISBN 0–333–99553–8

This book is printed on paper suitable for recycling
and made from fully managed and sustained forest sources.

A catalogue record for this book is available
from the British Library.

Library of Congress Cataloging-in-Publication Data

Noronha, Carlos.
    The theory of culture-specific total quality management : quality
    management in Chinese regions / Carlos Noronha.
        p.   cm.
    Includes bibliographical references and index.
    ISBN 0–333–99553–8
    1. Total quality management—China.   2. Total quality management—
    Taiwan   3. National characteristics, Chinese.   I. Title.

HD62.15 .N67 2002
658.4′013′0951—dc21
                                                          2002017696

10   9   8   7   6   5   4   3   2   1
11   10   09   08   07   06   05   04   03   02

Printed and bound in Great Britain by
Antony Rowe Limited
Chippenham, Wiltshire

To Florence with love

Contents

List of Tables

List of Figures

Acknowledgment

The author is grateful to Asian Productivity Organization, McGraw-Hill and Routledge (ITPS Ltd) for granting permission to reproduce the following: Table 5.1 from *TQM Practices in Asia-Pacific Firms* by Tomio Umeda published in 1996 (Asian Productivity Organization); Figure 2.1 from *Beyond Total Quality Management: Toward the Emerging Paradigm* by Greg Bounds, Lyle Yorks, Mel Adams and Gipsie Ranney published in 1994 (McGraw-Hill) and Figure 3.1 from *Consumer Behavior in China: Customer Satisfaction and Cultural Values* by Oliver H.M. Yau published in 1994 (Routledge (ITPS Ltd)).

Preface

This book is concerned with the influence of Chinese cultural values on the implementation of total quality management (TQM) in Chinese companies operating in three Chinese regions namely mainland China, Hong Kong, and Taiwan. The result of this study leads to the development of a theory of culture-specific TQM.

Total quality management is known to have begun mainly in Japan and the United States. The cultural values underlying the Japanese and the Americans are very different and even so, organizations embedded in different national cultures can succeed in quality management. It is argued that when TQM, as a transcendent and culture-free system, is being implemented in a certain cultural setting, it must accommodate to a certain extent the local culture, and a culture-specific TQM system is created.

Very few researchers have ever linked the study of TQM with national culture. There are several reasons. Firstly, TQM has long been practice-oriented and the audiences are frequently managers and practitioners rather than management theorists. A large research gap as to the theoretical constructs of TQM has yet to be filled given its popularity and relatedness with the management theories of leadership, organizational behavior, human resources, and so on. Secondly, TQM has remained a rather ambiguous concept and little convergence concerning its philosophical underpinnings has yet been established. It is clear that more comprehensive and holistic studies have to be conducted. Nevertheless, the most important reason is due to the way people see or want TQM and TQM research to be. A paradigmatic shift has to be made from the universalistic, ethnocentric, and manageralistic tradition to a more open, socio-culturally oriented, and unprejudiced approach to TQM. The present study aims at making a modest contribution to the current TQM literature by conjuring up different perspectives and views and going back to the basics of a socio-cultural approach to management phenomena.

Today, China represents one of the most important economies in the new century. The fast adaptation and absorption of new technologies and management concepts by the Chinese has never been surprising. When TQM is being implemented in these Chinese soils, a fusion between Chinese cultural values and TQM principles creates a TQM style pertaining to the Chinese people. Just as Japanese-style TQM and

American-style TQM can succeed, Chinese-style TQM can also excel. The study has paved way for understanding indigenous managerial psychology from a fresh perspective.

Many people are worth mentioning for their association, help, and support to the study. I am deeply grateful to Harukiyo Hasegawa of the University of Sheffield for providing me with constant support and guidance during my doctoral study. Also, without the help and encouragement from Nelson António of ISCTE in Lisbon, Oliver Yau of the City University of Hong Kong, Hideo Inohara of Sophia University, Gopal Kanji of Sheffield Hallam University, Robert Taylor of the University of Sheffield, the Mochimaru family in Saitama, and especially Tetsuo Abo of Teikyo University, my study would never have been possible. I am also indebted to all the managers who willingly sacrificed their time to answer my questionnaires and to enable me to complete the case studies. My thanks also go to my parents and my few but distinguished colleagues and friends, especially Zhao. Finally, I dedicate this work to Florence.

C.N.

1
Introduction

This book describes a study which examines the relationship between national culture and total quality management (TQM). A special reference to Chinese culture is made so as to identify the characteristics of a 'Chinese-style TQM' model. In this introductory chapter, it is argued that a 'culture-specific TQM' exists in contrast to the universalistic approach to TQM. The theoretical background for this argument is thus firstly presented. Then the objectives of the study are discussed. Finally, the methodology used in the study and the organization of the remaining chapters are outlined.

Theoretical foundation of the culture-specific TQM

During the past 20 years or so, TQM has been receiving widespread acceptance by the various sectors of the economy including manufacturing, service, government, health care, and education. This TQM phenomenon is worldwide. Probably few would disagree that no other management issue since Frederick Taylor's Scientific Management at the beginning of the century has created such a profound impact as what the TQM movement has achieved (Ross, 1993). Kanji (1990) has even described TQM as bringing about a second industrial revolution. Although in the popular press TQM is nowadays not as 'hot' as it was during the 1980s–1990s, academic interest in TQM has scarcely subsided (De Cock and Hipkin, 1997). In the 1990s, special issues of academic journals have devoted to the study of TQM. These include for example, *California Management Review* (1993), *Academy of Management Review* (1994), *Journal of Organizational Change Management* (1994), *Canadian Journal of Administrative Sciences* (1995), and *Employee Relations* (1995). As we are now in the new millenium, the continued publication of TQM-related papers in prestigious journals such as *Academy of Management Journal* (Douglas and Judge, 2001), *Journal of Management Studies* (Chiles and Choi, 2000), and *Organization Studies* (Knights and McCabe, 1999; Xu, 1999) proves that any claim that TQM is just another managerial fad is not fully justified.

Despite the continued attention given to it, Dean and Bowen (1994) pointed out that there is a need to stimulate more research on TQM at the theoretical level. Similarly, Waldman (1995) added that still relatively little academic research on TQM is done and the time is ripe for systematic work to proceed so as to achieve theory development. Stemming from its predecessor, statistical quality control, TQM has been practice-oriented, and the audiences have long been consultants and practitioners rather than management theorists. As such, researchers of various fields including public administration (Wilson and Durant, 1994), operations management (Handfield and Melnyk, 1998), economics (Chiles and Choi, 2000), and organizational studies (Douglas and Judge, 2001) have labeled TQM as atheoretical and are calling for more theory building research. Given its cross-functional nature, TQM actually has common roots with many familiar theories. For example, Hackman and Wageman (1995) approached TQM practices from the perspectives of behavioral science knowledge such as motivation, learning, and social system change. Powell (1995) examined TQM in terms of strategic management research and practice through the lens of firm-based resource theories. Cameron and Sine (1999) identified the key dimensions of quality culture based on organizational effectiveness theories. To encourage more theoretical inquiries into TQM will, in one way or the other, enhance our knowledge on management theories. As stressed by Whetten (1989), the most valuable fruit of theory development is reaped by borrowing different perspectives from other fields, thus challenging accepted theories and reconceptualizing our views on individuals, groups, and organizations. Furthermore, there is a need to develop theories in order to better understand the differences between successful and unsuccessful TQM implementations. Cameron and Sine (1999) pointed out that there have been a handful of documentation about failed TQM endeavors, and they attributed the lack of unanimity in the key dimensions of quality in the literature as an important reason for such failures. In fact, according to Peterson and Cameron (1995), only three per cent of the published articles on TQM up to 1995 in the United States were empirical in nature and not many have employed rigorous research methods. Thus, it can be seen that although TQM has been practiced so widely for a reasonably long period of time, it is still considered an ambiguous concept. The lack of theory development for TQM implies space for improving the integration of TQM research and practice. Although, it is until quite recently that some light has been shed on the theoretical underpinnings of TQM (e.g. Anderson *et al.*, 1994, 1995; Rungtusanatham *et al.*, 1998; Cameron and Sine, 1999; Chiles and Choi, 2000), the need to understand more about TQM from other related perspectives, sociological and cultural, should prove helpful towards the theoretical development of TQM as an essential organizational phenomenon.

Just as management theories are prescriptive rather than imperative, TQM theory should be contingent, varying according to the respective organizational context (Dean and Bowen, 1994). Total quality management should be regarded as a philosophy or a paradigm shift for the modern managers. One cannot simply view TQM as a set of imperative techniques or tools that can be directly applied to solve corporate problems in any setting. This mechanistic mode of TQM (Spencer, 1994) is only a limited part of the broad philosophy. Westphal *et al.* (1997) suggested that in approaching an administrative innovation such as TQM, institutional perspectives are suitable. They defined institutional perspectives as emphasizing on the role of social factors rather than economic or efficiency factors in driving organizational actions (p. 366). It is suggested here that in diagnosing the core elements of TQM such as customer focus, continuous improvement, and teamwork, the human factor must come to the fore. Human beings are nothing more than actors of their underlying cultural values. The cultural factor is obviously important in management theories of leadership, human resource management, and of course in TQM. In particular, the doctrines of the quality gurus such as Crosby (1979, 1986), Deming (1986), Feigenbaum (1991), Juran (1951, 1988, 1989, 1992, 1995), and the Japanese quality masters such as Imai (1991), Ishikawa (1985, 1990), and Mizuno (1979, 1988), have all emphasized the importance of cultural and human factors in successful quality management.

A shortcoming in the current theory development for TQM is the lack of empirical research to address the relationship between national culture and TQM in spite of anecdotal evidences that cultural influences are clear. This research gap has especially been pointed out by Chapman (1998) in *Total-Quality-Culture*, an internet discussion forum funded by the United Kingdom's Higher Education Funding Councils. It becomes obvious when one reviews the current literature of cultural influences on management. Two areas of interest to the present study have been frequently examined.

The first area is concerned with the impact of national cultures on organizations, or the shaping of organizational cultures by the respective national cultures. Hofstede's (1980) landmark study on work-related values addresses this area. His four, and later five major dimensions of culture namely, power distance, uncertainty avoidance, individualism versus collectivism, masculinity versus femininity, and long-term versus short-term orientation, were used to describe the work-related values of the people of different cultures. To a certain extent, organizational cultures can thus be explained by these national cultural dimensions. Another example is Schein's (1985) analysis of organizational culture. According to his three-level mode of organizational culture (basic underlying assumptions, espoused values, and artifacts), organizational culture is organization-specific and exists as a sub-culture of the higher level national culture. As argued by Hampden-Turner and Trompenaars (1993), corporations located in the same nation, region, ethnic group, or cultural group tend to share similar components of organizational culture. It is not difficult to locate a vast literature concerning the influences of national cultures on organizational cultures.

The second area of interest is on the reciprocal impacts of organizational cultures and TQM. In fact, no seminal publications to date with an authority comparable to that of Hofstede or Schein can be appropriately located. This could be largely due to the lack of TQM theory development as stated earlier. Nevertheless, many studies in this aspect have described a so-called quality culture (Hildebrandt *et al.*, 1991) or a total quality culture (Kanji and Yui, 1997), which integrates many of the principles and practices of TQM with the concepts of corporate culture (Deal and Kennedy, 1988) or organizational culture (Schein, 1985). For example, Kanji and Yui (1997) indicated that organizational culture is influenced by such dimensions as national background, ideology, and personality of the organizational members. Moreover, organizational culture can influence and can also be influenced by TQM principles. They also argued that a total quality culture leads to a higher level of customer delight.

Therefore, in order to facilitate TQM theory development based on a human and cultural perspective (as a branch of the institutional perspectives), it is necessary to connect the two areas of studies mentioned above. This will require research to explain TQM activities in a particular cultural setting as influenced by its national culture directly or through the respective organizational cultures. Though few in number, some attempts have touched on this area (e.g. Maccoby, 1994; Martinsons, 1996; Napier, 1997; Roney, 1997; Chen and Lu, 1998; Jenner *et al.*, 1998;

Lo, 1998, 1999; Martinsons and Hempel, 1998). However, most of them suffer from a rather low degree of representativeness or generalizability due to either the lack of empirical research or the incomprehensiveness of research findings. It is clear that more empirical studies taking a more holistic approach have to be conducted in order to narrow this obvious research gap.

In attempting to delineate the association between national culture and TQM, it appears insightful here to draw upon the classical socio-logical theory of an action system. According to Parsons (1951: 4), the object world can be classified into three classes of social objects: (1) the 'social' referring to the actor or the collectivity; (2) the 'physical' refer-ring to entities which do not interact with the actor; and (3) the 'cul-tural' referring to symbolic elements of the cultural tradition not internalized as constitutive elements of the actor's personality. A culture emerges and becomes part of an action system of the actor when symbolic systems mediate communication among actors (p. 5). Thus a social system or a partial social system functions when a plurality of individual actors interact through commonly understood and shared cultural symbols. A value is therefore, defined as an element of a shared symbolic system which serves as a standard for selection among alternative orientations intrinsically open in a certain situation. Through such a mechanism, value orientation serves as a device in articulating cultural traditions into an action system (p. 12).

Putting such an understanding of value orientation into the context of an economic organization, Parsons further elaborated that the value orientation of the organization (the sub-value system) is always defined by that of the social system (a higher order or super-ordinate value system). Unless the organization is deviant or disintegrated from the super-ordinate system, the value system of the organization must imply basic acceptance of the more generalized values of the super-ordinate system (Parsons, 1956: 67). This value system in turn formulates the operative codes which govern the organization in making organizational policies as well as allocative and coordination decisions and actions. Thus, we are reassured of the position that the everyday organizational activities of organizational members are, to a certain extent, governed by such underlying value orientations, or in other words, cultural values.

Applying this Parsonian framework to the attempt to associate national culture and TQM, a proposition can thus be stated. The national culture (the super-ordinate value system) operates as an influence on the organ-izational culture (the sub-value system) which formulates the operative codes in putting TQM into concrete actions. However, based on the transcendent view (Garvin, 1988), which regards quality as a property difficult to define and can be understood only through experience, TQM appears to be itself a set of philosophy with its own existence. Thus, when implementing TQM in a particular cultural setting, the fusion effect of the respective national culture and TQM as a culture itself is of great importance.

This fusion effect can be analyzed and further elaborated by means of an 'emic–etic' analysis. Derived from linguistics, Pike (1954) used the emic–etic concept to describe human behaviors across cultures. In simple terms, emics refer to specifics valid only for one culture or one culturally defined class of people. On the other hand, etics refer to universalities across different cultures. This emic–etic theory was then applied to devise approaches for cross-cultural studies. Berry (1990) defined a three-step approach. 'Imposed etic' when a researcher begins to analyze a culture from his or her own cultural viewpoint, 'emic' when the researcher discovers principles specific only to a particular culture, and 'derived etic' when universalities are discovered through a comparison of the imposed etics and emics. This three-step approach enjoys much popularity among cross-cultural researchers. Uemura (1998) employed the emic–etic analysis to explain the transferability of Japanese-style management overseas. Drawing largely from Abo's (1994) study on the Japanese transplants in America, Uemura argued that two emic systems (e.g. full Japanese model as emic A and full American model as emic B) when put together will give rise to a hybrid system (e.g. Japanese–American hybrid C) but not a full absorption of one by the other. Three possible combinations may arise, a high diversity hybrid, a middle diversity hybrid, or a low diversity hybrid. Uemura further used Rugman's (1981) internalization theory and argued that when two emic systems contact each other, the more advantageous system will be transferred to the other when there is little protection barrier. On the other hand, when there is little etics or commonalities, a drastic change will occur.

Uemura's theory is in line with Abo's argument. Abo pointed out that there has been a strong impression that Japanese-style management concerns characteristics peculiar to the Japanese culture and it seems that the more emphasis people place on linking management theory and culture, the more limited is the potential for its international transfer. However, given the ongoing debate in reality, the strong link between management theory and culture cannot be ignored. It essentially becomes a matter of recognizing that cultural trends lend themselves to a variety of expressions in different periods and under changing conditions. Also, certain aspects of culture can be isolated in terms of quantitative differences which may be compared internationally. As a result, a meaningful study of international transfer must identify which aspects of the system are most subject to change, and evaluate the degree of change that takes place (Abo, 1994: 14–15). In other words, the socio-cultural influence on any management system is an undeniable element and effective transfer of systems must adapt the technology to the local country principally defined by its socio-cultural background (p. 235).

The emic–etic theory that Uemura has pointed out or the 'application–adaptation' model of Abo both refer to the fusion of two management systems, which are embedded in two distinct national cultures. The effect of the fusion or the hybrid thus depends on the commonalities between the two systems. Now, if one applies the emic–etic theory to the relationship between national culture and TQM, the situation is slightly different. The national culture in question represents a particular set of value orientations pertaining to a country, for example, China. On the other hand, TQM itself can also be regarded as a culture possessing its own emic aspects. Here the point is that TQM itself as a culture does not incline toward any particular country or national culture. Total quality management as a culture itself is transcendent (Garvin, 1988). For example, Roney (1997), in her analysis of implementing TQM in Poland, underscored that TQM itself is embedded with its own set of cultural beliefs, norms, values, and assumptions. This is consistent with Beyer *et al.*'s description of TQM as a 'pre-packaged culture' (Beyer *et al.*, 1996; cited in Roney, 1997). Although, Roney agreed that TQM can be regarded as a culture itself, she also pointed out that TQM is embedded with cultural values and assumptions which are consistent with its culture of origin, which is predominantly Japanese. This statement is in contrast with the transcendent characteristic of TQM. If TQM itself is more consistent with Japanese culture, it means that when TQM is fused together with a distinct culture, say, American management system, a high diversity hybrid will arise and this may inhibit the effective implementation of TQM. This is probably not the case. For instance, Emery (1978; cited in Napier, 1997) believed that the quality movement could be emulated wherever there are human beings, and it is not a peculiar product of Japanese culture.

It is clear that TQM is being successfully implemented in Western companies which prize individual autonomy highly as well as in Asian companies which value good interpersonal relationships rather than individual rights (Maccoby, 1994). In other words, TQM as a culture itself is not country specific. Rather, TQM is mutable and can quickly adapt to the respective national culture in question. Thus, for TQM to succeed in America, an American-style TQM influenced by the American culture must be formed. For TQM to succeed in Japan, Japanese-style TQM, as what Ishikawa (1985) had coined, must appear. In terms of the present study, for TQM to be effectively implemented in Chinese societies, there must be a Chinese-style TQM. However, one should not wipe out the possibility that there may exist certain commonalities or etic aspects among these three hybrids. American-style TQM, Japanese-style TQM, and Chinese-style TQM should be regarded as three distinct hybrids resulting from the fusion of TQM with the respective national cultures. The existence of the culture-specific TQM echoes the argument of Boyer (1998) and Hasegawa (1998) that hybridization or hybrid management is a principle of genesis or transformation, resulting in a distinct system through interactions with the local social and cultural setting.

Ishikawa (1985) pointed out that there are many ways of looking at Japan's post-war economic miracles, but in the final analysis, human and cultural factors are most important. Japanese-style management has somehow found the secret of harnessing the energy of its people very effectively. This has been accomplished in large measures by a device called TQM. As such, Japanese-style TQM and Japanese production systems are highly influenced by Japanese culture (Fröhner and Iwata, 1996). On the other hand, Clegg *et al.* (1986: 12–13) have identified four Confucian traits to be active among Chinese societies: (1) Socialization within the family unit in such a way to promote sobriety, education, and seriousness about tasks, job, family, and obligations; (2) a tendency to help the group; (3) a sense of hierarchy; and (4) a sense of complementarity of relations. If Ishikawa's argument was true for the case of Japan, Chinese regions can also achieve world class industrial performance through the creation of a distinct Chinese-style TQM embedded in these important indigenous cultural traits. Just as Japanese-style and American-style TQM can succeed, Chinese-style TQM can also do so.

Chinese culture has been chosen as the subject in the present study. The reason is that in the process of globalization of business today, mainland China and the overseas Chinese regions such as Hong Kong and Taiwan have been regarded as lands of opportunities and potentials. For example, the national productivity indices of 18 Asian countries were topped by Taiwan, Singapore the third, and Hong Kong fourth (APO, 1997). Also, the recent agenda of mainland China joining the World Trade Organizations has undoubtedly affirmed China as an important player of the world economy. The fast adaptation and absorption of new technologies and management concepts by the Chinese is not and has never been surprising. Nowadays many regard the label of 'made in Hong Kong' or 'made in Taiwan' as a sign of high quality which can compete with their Western counterparts.

These Chinese regions have also been feverishly pursuing TQM activities and are gradually maturing. In Taiwan, the history of quality activities can be traced back to the early 1970s. The movement matured mainly from 1988 onwards, when the government-sponsored national quality promotion program played a vital role in converting Taiwan's enterprise from being production-driven to being customer-driven (Lee *et al.*, 1996: 128). In Hong Kong, the quality movement also started during the 1970s with the establishment of the Hong Kong Productivity Council, the Hong Kong Quality Assurance Agency, and other quality conscious bodies. Most companies joining the quality movement now see quality, at least in the form of a certified quality management system like the ISO 9000, as a minimum qualification for survival (Cheng, 1996: 167; Lee, 1998). In the case of mainland China, the open door policy in the late 1970s laid the cornerstone for its industrial and economic development today. Although slower than its Asian counterparts, quality consciousness has increasingly become the focal point of business in China today. Followed by the rapid and large-scale foreign direct investment of multinational companies and the installation of the China State Bureau for Technical Standards implying an initiative from the central authority, China has joined the league of quality movement in Asia.

It is hoped that the present study will provide a modest contribution towards the theoretical and practical aspects of TQM implementation. Theoretically, the study aims to develop a culture-specific TQM model which characterizes the transcendent and mutable forms of TQM itself as a self-existing set of philosophy in line with the cultural mode of organizations. Grounded on sociological and psychological processes, the culture-specific model helps to better understand and to raise the awareness of cultural influences on organizations. There have been many reports on the failure of TQM programs due to the direct implementation of techniques imported from foreign soil. However, the question lies on what kind of adaptations have to be made for effective implementation. Also, when adaptations are being made, which cultural value is more sensitive to TQM and as such how should TQM activities be modeled in order to suit the culture? By referring to the model as suggested in this study, practitioners will be able to grasp a basic understanding of the association between cultural values and TQM and can thus formulate better strategies for modeling their own TQM implementations.

Research objectives

From what has been presented above, the need for more comprehensive studies relating culture, especially Chinese culture, and TQM is justified. In this exploratory study, Chinese cultural values and TQM as key ingredients to organizational development, are extensively investigated based on three Chinese regions. The study utilizes structural equation modeling to analyze the complex inter-relationships among Chinese cultural values and elements of TQM.

In essence, the first primary objective of this study is to add to the nascent literature of national cultural influence on TQM so as to make a modest contribution to the theory development of TQM. In this respect, the cultural values of the Chinese TQM companies are viewed as partial social systems operating within a general super-ordinate society. Secondly, the study hopes to broaden the understanding of TQM companies currently operating in three Chinese regions namely, mainland China, Hong Kong, and Taiwan. Finally, it is hoped to generate a theoretical culture-specific TQM model, which enables companies to better understand their positions and to provide a sign of culture-awareness when implementing TQM.

Methodology of the study and structure of the book

The methodology employed for this empirical study involves three distinctive phases. The first phase is to assess the current TQM practices of companies in mainland China, Hong Kong, and Taiwan which have attained ISO 9000 certifications. Three samples of ISO 9000 companies in the three regions with at least three years of certification history were obtained from an administration of mailed questionnaires. For the sake of obtaining matched samples, companies which have obtained ISO 9000 certifications for over three years are assumed to be practicing TQM, although it is known that ISO 9000 is only one of the many aspects of TQM. Despite justifications of this assumption given in Chapter 2, this remains a limitation of the study.

Two research instruments, in the form of attitudinal questionnaires, were administered among the quality managers or officers of the sampled companies in this phase: (1) A modified 73-item version of the 'Quality and Productivity Self-Assessment Guide for Defense Organizations version 1.0' originally developed by the US Department of Defense (DoD, 1992). The original English instrument was translated into Chinese and was followed by a process of back-translation; and (2) A 45-item

Chinese Cultural Value instrument developed by Yau (1994). In this case, the original Chinese version supplied by the author was administered. 473, 613, and 1200 sets of instruments were sent to companies in mainland China, Hong Kong, and Taiwan respectively. From the three regions 117, 79, and 189 useable questionnaires were returned respectively. The Statistical Package for the Social Sciences (SPSS 8.0) was utilized to analyze the data. Factor analysis was applied to the data to extract inputs for the second phase of the study.

The second phase of the study involves the generation of a comprehensive model explaining the inter-relationships among the extracted factors. Here, the structural equation modeling software AMOS 3.62 otherwise known as Analysis of Moment Structure (Arbuckle, 1997) was employed. The parameters of the model and the entire model itself were then subject to various tests of significance and goodness of fit.

The final phase involves presenting three qualitative case studies of ISO 9000 companies operating in Hong Kong and mainland China to complement the quantitative findings in the previous phases. The findings of the quantitative and the qualitative inquiries were then cross-analyzed in order to identify the special characteristics of a Chinese-style TQM model in the form of a schematic framework.

A review of relevant literature on TQM is presented in Chapter 2. A general framework of TQM is drawn based on the doctrines of renowned American and Japanese quality experts. Related issues such as ISO 9000 certification and the impact of TQM on firm performance are also reported. Chapter 3 carries a discussion on cultural values. Several representative definitions are reviewed, followed by an exposition of Chinese cultural values. Chapter 4 sets the background for the hypothesized culture-specific TQM model. Relevant studies are reported, compared, and criticized. The theoretical framework of the culture-specific TQM is then developed.

Chapter 5, Research Methodology, firstly identifies the samples of the study. Then, the origin and structure of the research instruments are explained. Finally, a hypothesized model explaining the relationships between TQM and Chinese cultural values is proposed.

In Chapter 6, Data Analysis and results, the responses to the TQM survey and the Chinese cultural value survey are reported and subjected to several statistical processes. The structural equation model suggesting the relationships between TQM and Chinese cultural values is then tested.

In Chapter 7, three case studies reporting ISO 9000 companies operating in Hong Kong and mainland China are presented. The cases help to complement and to cross-validate the quantitative findings and to suggest the characteristics of a Chinese-style TQM model.

Finally, Chapter 8 presents the conclusions and a brief summary of the study. Contributions and limitations as well as some recommendations for further research are also discussed.

2
Quality and TQM

In this chapter, three major areas of interest are covered. Firstly, the concept of quality and the definition of TQM are discussed leading to a suggested framework for TQM. Secondly, ISO 9000 certification as a TQM implementation issue is presented. Finally, the impact of TQM on firm performance is reviewed. The chapter aims to serve as a comprehensive literature review of quality and TQM for the reader.

Total quality management

This section firstly provides the concept of quality. Then, several definitions of TQM are reviewed and their essentials extracted. Finally, the framework for TQM used in the present study is explained.

The concept of quality

Defining quality is a difficult task because there exist many different interpretations. Quality can be understood as continuous improvement. Quality can mean excellence. Quality can mean meeting customer requirements. Hansen (2001: 209) lamented that it is unfortunate that until today the concept of quality appears fragmented and ambiguous in literature as well as in practice. A literature search conducted by him has identified five major definitions namely, quality as an excellent product, quality as value, quality as the consumers perceive it, quality as adaptation to expectations, and quality as adaptation to technical specifications. Assessing the perceptions from the producers' and the consumers' criteria and over different industries, his empirical investigation revealed little consensus on the five definitions. Although it has been pointed out earlier that unanimity of the concept may have led to many failed TQM efforts, it is time for both companies and consumers to make a paradigm shift on how to understand the meaning of quality. Hansen urged for a clearer definition of quality but more importantly, the specific context surrounding the definition must be clearly understood. Arguing for standardization of the concept or one single interpretation is indeed unrealistic. Similarly, treating quality or TQM as a discrete phenomenon does not lead to conclusive evidence in the literature (Westphal *et al.*, 1997; Douglas and Judge, 2001). Knights and McCabe (1997) have vividly illustrated this by a case study of a retail bank. When the strategic intentions of the bank were to improve customer services and to render its culture more consistent with that aim, a 'conformance to requirements' (Crosby, 1979) approach to quality is ill-suited to either ends because of its neglect of both customers and culture (Knights and McCabe, 1997: 381). Thus, the definition of quality is not only geared towards the surrounding context, the multiple users, but also the intention of the organization.

For the purpose of the present study, quality has to be approached from a human and cultural perspective. A general or first-order definition is more suitable than specific ones which are for specific contexts. A fundamental concept of quality is Garvin's transcendent view on quality. Under this view, quality is defined as 'innate excellence, both absolute and universally recognizable, a mark of uncompromising standards and high achievement' (Garvin, 1988: 41). Although such a definition is clearly abstract and too vague for practical purposes, the transcendent view acts as an ultimate guiding principle under which pragmatic definitions of quality based on product (e.g. minimization of product variability), manufacturing (e.g. engineering and manufacturing practices), user (e.g. customer orientation), and value (e.g. cost and price) can be devised (pp. 39–48).

In any organization, based on the transcendent view on quality, quality is created by a quality culture. Goetsch and Davis (1994: 122) defined a quality culture as 'an organizational value system which results in an environment that is conducive to the establishment and continual improvement of quality and it consists of values, traditions, procedures, and expectations that promote quality'. Any specific quality processes, quality management tools, and quality results or outcomes should be viewed as subsets of the broad guiding principle. The transcendent view on quality as a cultural variable coincides with the nature of management theory which is contingent rather than imperative. Just as Cameron and Sine (1999: 10) have argued, treating quality as a cultural variable has the advantage of diminishing the ambiguity and inconsistency associated with the multiple definitions and dimensions of quality.

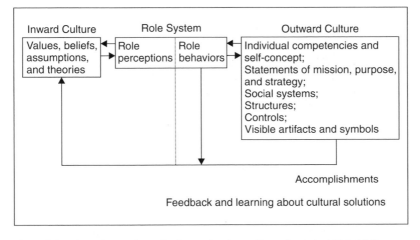

Figure 2.1 The relationship of roles and culture (Bounds *et al.*, 1994: 134).

The management practices congruent with the principles of a quality culture focus on building internalization of quality values in all organizational members (Bright and Cooper, 1993: 22). Throughout the organization, the role of management is essential in putting the culture at work by concretizing the transcendent view on quality. Figure 2.1 is important for understanding how management bridges the gap between inward culture and managerial performance. Here, the responsibility of management is to function on the middle ground, that is, the role systems. Role perceptions reside in the minds of people (inward culture) as beliefs about what one is responsible for doing. If conditions are right, these perceptions lead to role behaviors (outward culture), which are actions to accomplish the role perceptions (Bounds *et al.*, 1994: 134–5). In creating a quality culture in an organization, the transcendent view on quality must be instilled in the inward culture. The managerial role of the leaders is to transform the principle into outward culture elements, concretizing them into structures and actions such as quality processes, quality methods, and quality results.

Shuster's (1990) approach to defining quality can be seen supportive to this argument. He stressed that individual people is an indispensable element in any quality framework. It is the individual who initiates a quality process, which results in outcomes, creating consequences to be experienced by the individual again. It is clear here that a quality

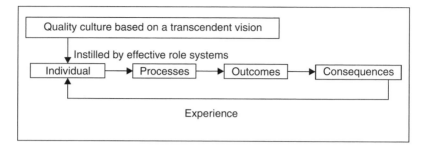

Figure 2.2   The concept of quality.

culture is the product of people and it must be based on some guiding principles or visions best expressed from a transcendent viewpoint. Throughout the present study, the transcendent approach to quality is followed. Any pragmatic aspects of quality are seen as products of this central vision, and they are concretized into actions by effective role systems of the management. Figure 2.2 depicts the concept of quality based on the transcendent and cultural viewpoint.

Definitions of TQM

It is rather difficult to mark the birth of quality control historically. Juran (1989) stated that strategies for managing quality have already been adopted since mankind's early civilization. For example, the inspection of incoming food. However, it would be much more practical to mark the birth of quality control since the time Frederick Taylor introduced scientific management in around 1875 when the concept of mass production and the division of labor began to appear in the American industrial sector (DeVor *et al.*, 1992: 8). Walter Shewhart marked another important era of quality development in 1925 when he developed the statistical approach to study manufacturing process variations (Shewhart, 1931). Statistical process control, as it was then named, was used extensively during the Second World War for military purpose.

Nevertheless, many prefer to mark the birth of quality control during the post-war Japan period from 1945 onwards when the General Head-quarters led by MacArthur established the Civil Communication Section with the objective of reviving the infrastructure of Japan ruined by the war. In 1946, the Union of Japanese Scientists and Engineers (JUSE) was established, followed by a national campaign of training in quality control methods. In 1950, William Edwards Deming visited Japan and offered seminars on statistical process control for Japanese industrialists. This was quickly followed by the visit of another American quality expert, Joseph Juran in 1954 whose teachings had placed more emphasis on top management leadership rather than statistical methods. Quality control development in Japan fostered rapidly on a nationwide scope.

The late 1970s and early 1980s witnessed the rapid evolution of quality management systems in the West, especially the United States. This was largely due to the fact that the Japanese were able to integrate many of the American concepts of quality control into their own system, creating a unique Japanese-style total quality control widely known as TQC. In concrete terms, Japan was able to sustain two oil crises followed by the large-scale export of economical motor vehicles and electronic appliances. The combination of increased consumer interest in quality and foreign competition have forced American management to become more concerned with quality (Gitlow, 1994: 6). It is often said that quality management was reimported to the United States from Japan. Ishikawa (1985) even stated that Japan had transformed quality control into a new product, which was then widely exported to nations overseas and became a worldwide phenomenon.

Dale *et al.* (1990: 3–4) suggested that the evolution of quality systems can be roughly divided into four stages namely, inspection, quality control, quality assurance, and total quality management. As the focus on customer satisfaction and employee involvement were built into the concept of sole quality control or quality assurance, the term total quality management or TQM, as it is often called, began to replace TQC (Harris, 1995). Today, TQM is practiced widely by all kinds of organizations worldwide, no matter manufacturing or service, large or small. Total quality management has been accepted as a viable and effective management system, confined not only to the inspection department, but to the entire organization (Ishikawa, 1985: 20–1). Hackman and Wagemen (1995: 339) concluded that TQM is a set of powerful interventions wrapped in a highly attractive package which will sustain over time, if researchers and practitioners continuously improve and illuminate this provocative philosophy. A very important point to note in the transformation from quality control to TQM is the integration of human factors into a system which was once thought of as totally technical and mechanical. An examination of the various definitions of TQC or TQM below makes the point clear.

Apart from Kaoru Ishikawa in Japan, Armand Feigenbaum was perhaps the first to coin the term 'Total Quality Control (TQC)' in the United States. According to his definition, TQC is 'an effective system for integrating the quality development, quality maintenance, and quality improvement efforts of the various groups in an organization so as to enable marketing, engineering, production, and service at the most economical levels which allow for full customer satisfaction' (Feigenbaum, 1991: 6). His definition has stressed the importance of an organization-wide impact.

In Japan, Shigeru Mizuno stated that TQC has to involve everyone and all activities from corporate management to entry-level workers in everything from design to manufacturing, inspection, sales, procurement, energy management, accounting, and personnel (Mizuno, 1988: 17). Total quality control is undoubtedly an integrative strategic framework of any organization. According to JUSE, TQC requires that from top to bottom in a company, each person in each department must be quality minded (Dale, 1994: 80). The essence is to stress the 'T' in TQC. That is to say, quality is everybody's job. Participation must become company-wide (Ishikawa, 1985: 21).

The US Department of Defense suggested TQM as both a philosophy and a set of guiding principles that represent the foundation of a continuously improving organization. Their definition of TQM is 'a disciplined management process under the leadership of the top executive, involving everyone in the organization in a cooperative effort to achieve a quality product or service through continuous process improvement combined with continuous life cycle cost reduction to satisfy customer needs and maximize combat capability' (DoD, 1990). Again, it is seen that the human factor plays a major role in TQM. The activity of everyone participating in the achievement of one objective is especially significant and valuable, leading to their taking ownership of TQM (Umeda, 1996: 4).

At the international level, the International Organization for Standardization defines quality management as the responsibility of all levels of management but must be led by top management. Its implementation involves all members of the organization (ISO, 1994a: 14).

Kanji's general definition of TQM serves as a good summary of the above discussions. According to him, 'Quality' is to satisfy customers' requirements continually; 'Total Quality' is to achieve quality at low cost; 'Total Quality Management' is to obtain total quality by involving everyone's daily commitment (Kanji, 1990: 5). In order to develop the TQM process, the organization has to be guided by seven basic rules of actions: (1) The approach: management-led; (2) the scope: company-wide; (3) the scale: everyone is responsible for quality; (4) the philosophy: prevention not detection; (5) the standard: right first time; (6) the control: cost of quality; and (7) the theme: continuous improvement (p. 7).

A point of particular interest to the present study is that he also argued that organizations in the United States did not follow completely the Japanese method in developing quality processes. Instead they have considered their country's basic cultural issues and have thus developed their own quality culture. This important point has been rejoined by Powell's (1995) empirical study which stated that most of the 'hard' features of TQM, like process management and benchmarking do not necessarily produce advantages for the firm. Rather, certain tacit and behavioral features such as organizational culture as influenced by the respective national culture can produce substantial advantages.

TQM according to the Gurus

The doctrines of selected American and Japanese quality gurus are reviewed in this section. In line with this study's human and cultural approach to TQM, the review emphasizes on what the quality experts have to say on human and cultural issues influencing TQM.

William E. Deming

The early teachings of Deming during his visits to Japan in the 1950s placed a lot of emphasis on the use of statistical process control. At the same time, he strongly emphasized the importance of human factors in quality management. He believed in worker participation in decision-making, and the responsibility of management is to help people work smarter, not harder (Brocka and Brocka, 1992: 65). Deming stressed that Western-style management must undergo a transformation which can only be accomplished by man, not by hardware (Deming, 1986: 18). The famous Deming's 14 points for management have been the central guidance for many quality organizations. These 14 points represent generalizations drawn from Deming's own consulting experience with Japanese and American companies spanning a gradual process of four decades (Anderson *et al.*, 1994: 474). They are given here in summarized headings: (1) create constancy of purpose; (2) adopt new management philosophy; (3) cease dependence on mass inspection; (4) minimize total cost; (5) improve constantly and forever; (6) institute on-job training; (7) institute leadership; (8) eliminate fear; (9) eliminate departmental barriers; (10) eliminate slogans, exhortations, and targets; (11) eliminate work standards and management by objective; (12) abolish annual or merit rating; (13) institute education and self-improvement programs; and (14) institute organization-wide commitment. It can be seen that all the points have put tremendous emphasis on human factors and relations.

In particular, Deming called for the instillation of a new philosophy (points 1 and 2). This can only be achieved when top management demonstrates a genuine interest and commitment for life to quality and productivity. Furthermore, external human relations are essential. For example, he suggested that minimization of total costs can be achieved by building a long-term relationship of loyalty and trust with a single supplier (point 4). Deming also adopted Shewhart's plan-do-check-act (PDCA) cycle for continuous improvement (point 5). The PDCA cycle should be viewed as an ongoing and constant learning process without end. Furthermore, Deming advocated the humanization of management through leadership, training, teamwork, and elimination of fear (points 6, 7, 8, 9, 10, and 13). Pride of workmanship which increases the job satisfaction of workers is crucial (points 11 and 12). In brief, the Deming management methods call for vision and philosophy, learning, and humanization in the quality organization.

Joseph M. Juran

Juran's doctrines are directed at top management commitment and leadership. He called upper management amateurs and felt it is necessary to convert them into professionals through a cultural change which requires their own active participation (Juran, 1992: 13). In fact, Juran's teachings have emphasized a lot on the concept of cultural patterns proposed by the anthropologists Margaret Mead and Ruth Benedict. According to him, every organization is also a human society and evolves a pattern of beliefs, habits, practices, and values. Any change in this cultural pattern is deemed to bring in threats and resistance (pp. 77–8, 429–33). It is thus the responsibility of the upper management to lead a cultural change in the organization and to unfreeze resistance to change.

Juran recommended very humanistic ways in the progression of a cultural change. For example: (1) participation; (2) stripping off unnecessary technical and cultural baggage; (3) working with leadership; (4) treating people with dignity; (5) minimizing the impacts of cultural change; (6) putting oneself in other's shoes; (7) making use of humanistic ways such as persuasion and facilitation (Juran, 1995: 169–73). Furthermore, he believed that managerial breakthrough is by the acquisition of new knowledge through never-ending training. Generally speaking, Juran is a firm believer of the cultural approach to managing quality in organizations.

Armand V. Feigenbaum

Feigenbaum's doctrines are basically on the importance of organization-wide participation in TQM. He underscored that truly effective TQM enters deeply into the fundamental concepts of an organization and everyone in an organization, from top level managers to production line workers, must involve personally (Feigenbaum, 1991: 13). Feigenbaum also emphasized the importance of human factors in achieving total commitment. For example, some essential issues include ongoing quality education, creation of quality mindedness, participation based on behavioral science principles, formalized training in quality management, and effective communication within the organization (pp. 200–29). Nevertheless, Feigenbaum's doctrine on quality management can be summarized in his three steps to quality namely, organizational commitment, modern quality technology, and quality leadership (Brocka and Brocka, 1992: 73).

Philip B. Crosby

Crosby equates quality management with prevention (Brocka and Brocka, 1992: 61). He is best known for his advocacy on 'zero defect', which focuses on changing the attitudes and behaviors of the employees since he attributes quality problems to the lack of attention to details (Harris, 1995: 96). He claims that three important elements namely, determination, education, and implementation are the 'quality vaccine' for organizations striving for quality. Again, it is not difficult to notice that his emphasis is again on human factors. Determination is achieved only through top management commitment. Education and implementation both require organization-wide participation. Most important of all, Crosby stresses that an organization must learn and all its members must also learn to take appropriate roles. Furthermore, he has suggested 14 points for management similar to those of Deming's. Some important points include long-term management commitment, cross-departmental collaborations, zero defects, and organization-wide participation and involvement (Crosby, 1979).

Kaoru Ishikawa

Often known as the father of Japanese-style TQC, Ishikawa's teachings were extremely important to the maturity of Japan's quality movement. Similar to Deming, Ishikawa was famous for his teachings of statistical methods in quality control. During the 1960s and 1970s, his book *Hinshitsu kanri nyumon* (Ishikawa, 1964) published by JUSE and later translated into English as *Introduction to Quality Control* (Ishikawa, 1990) was almost treated as the bible for manufacturing companies in Japan. The popular 'seven tools' introduced in the book namely, the Pareto chart, fishbone diagram, histogram, check sheet, scatter diagram, flowchart, and control chart, are practiced worldwide. However, statistical methods were not Ishikawa's only contribution to the quality movement. He was probably the first in Japan to underscore the human factor in managing quality. For example, the quality control circle (QCC), which is regarded as one of the most powerful TQM interventions, was developed by Ishikawa. According to him, QCCs are not only devices for generating employee suggestions. Quality control circle activities aim at much higher level achievements such as respect for humanity and building a worthwhile and pleasant workplace through fully unleashing human capabilities (Ishikawa, 1985: 140). True quality requires a completely new vision, leadership, and commitment of management (pp. 121–36).

Ishikawa also had a lot to say about the cultural aspects of TQM. In explaining the difference between Japanese and Western experiences in quality, he stressed that quality control activities cannot be conducted in a social and cultural vacuum, and they have to develop within the framework of different societies and cultures (p. 23). In particular, several cultural aspects that he had suggested appear to be very important to the present study.

Firstly, he stated that Japan's vertical society implies strong line relationships among manufacturing, design, marketing, and purchasing activities. On the other hand, due to the characteristics of a vertical society, staff functions including quality control requires more improvement (p. 24). Secondly, he believed that elitism and class consciousness have been inhibiting the quality movement in certain countries such as France and Indonesia. He even attributed elitism akin to Taylorism, which inhibits true total participation in the organization (pp. 25–6). Thirdly, he also believed that countries which use the Chinese script or Japanese *kanji* in writing generally possess a workforce which is more willing to learn and diligent, and this could associate directly or indirectly with the success of quality activities (p. 29). This argument has been restated recently by Fröhner and Iwata (1996) in their study of the Japanese production systems. They concluded that due to the difficulties associated with the writing of *kanji*, various concepts including TQM, *kaizen, kanban,* and *poka-yoke* have been developed to meet a high standard of productivity (p. 217). As such, the principles of Japanese production systems are highly influenced by unique elements of the Japanese culture (p. 211). A deeper understanding of specific cultural elements is required in order to convert the theory of organization into practice (p. 216). Fourthly, Japan as a homogeneous nation, provides easier communication when conducting quality activities. Ishikawa (1985: 29–30) cited an example of a German factory which had to use eight different languages for communication. Also, education has been a key point in the success of Japan's quality movement. Ishikawa stressed that the love of education since the Meiji Restoration had a strong influence on providing a workforce which is literate and shows high aptitude for mathematics. Therefore, educating people in Japan on quality techniques and concepts has been much easier than in other countries with high illiteracy (p. 30). Finally, Ishikawa believed in the influence of religion on the implementation of quality activities. He claimed that trust among people can be easily achieved because according to the teachings of Confucianism and Buddhism, man is by nature good. He compared this with the management philosophy of Western nations which has not been showing trust among workers in organizations (pp. 31–2). Xu (1999: 662, 665) noticed that Ishikawa's assertion on the Japanese Confucian tradition which shaped Japanese attitudes and their capacity for actions has conditioned the ways of organizing TQC in a uniquely Japanese way. This is clearly reflected in the title of Ishikawa's 1985 publication *What is Quality Control? The Japanese Way*.

Although some may not agree totally with what Ishikawa had stated especially with his argument concerning religion, what is important here is that he firmly believed that culture does have a strong influence on quality management activities. This is in line with the central object of investigation in the present study.

Genichi Taguchi

Taguchi is well-known for his statistical engineering approach to quality control which encompasses a number of relatively advanced mathematical techniques such as the use of experimental design for quality control. The 'Taguchi method', as it is commonly called for convenience, is regarded as a further step in traditional statistical process control and is employed by many manufacturing companies worldwide. His central philosophy to the definition of quality is in stark contrast to common concepts such as 'fitness for use', 'conformance to requirements' or 'customer satisfaction' circulated in the West. His definition is that a lack of quality represents a 'loss to society' (Taguchi, 1986). This 'loss to society' is then measured by a 'loss function', a mathematical expression helpful for decision-makers in understanding the impact of quality on monetary profitability and loss.

What is important in terms of Taguchi's teachings to the present study is that his methods, although purely mathematical in nature, do have a cultural aspect. For example, his definition of 'loss to society' is obviously culturally oriented, reflecting two common oriental values namely, aspiration for perfectionism and working for the collective good (Goh,

1993: 188). While American quality gurus talk about pleasing the customer, Taguchi thinks of helping society, a manifestation of Japanese cultural habits that reflect the inclination towards uniformity, harmony, and predictability (p. 195). Also, Taguchi suggested the use of standard orthogonal arrays, liner graphs, and interaction tables in his method. This approach has been said to reflect the Japanese cultural propensity for uniformity and doing things by standard examples (p. 194).

A framework for TQM

Hackman and Wageman (1995: 310–11) identified four major assumptions in the TQM philosophy. Firstly, quality is assumed to be less costly than poor workmanship and is essential for the long-term survival of the organization. Secondly, employees naturally care about quality and will take initiatives to improve it as long as they are provided with the tools and training that are needed and are respected by management. Thirdly, organizations are systems of highly interdependent parts, and the problems they face cross traditional function lines. Lastly, quality is viewed as ultimately and inescapably the responsibility of top management. The first assumption is in line with the transcendent view on quality because quality should be viewed as an ongoing pursuit in the life of any organization. The second, third, and last assumptions are central to the major theme of the present study. That is to say, the importance of the human factor and subsequently, cultural factors, in TQM activities.

In line with the human and cultural explanation of Shuster's (1990) approach to quality described earlier, a framework for TQM has to be process-oriented. A basic concept underlying TQM is the PDCA cycle repeatedly stressed by the quality masters such as Shewhart (1931), Ishikawa (1985), Deming (1986), and Imai (1991). It is out of this fundamental concept that they commonly advocate the use of process-management heuristics such as flowcharts and cause-and-effect diagrams in enhancing TQM activities (Hackman and Wageman, 1995: 314). An excellent example of a process model of TQM is that suggested by the US Department of Defense (DoD, 1990). This model has been the basis of the prestigious Malcom Baldrige National Quality Award in the United States and also the ISO 9000 international quality standards. It is depicted in Figure 2.3.

The model can be explained by four inter-related quality dimensions, namely: (1) quality climate (step 1); (2) quality processes (steps 2 and 3); (3) quality methods (steps 4 and 5); and (4) quality results (steps 6 and 7). These four dimensions are in line with the four major sections

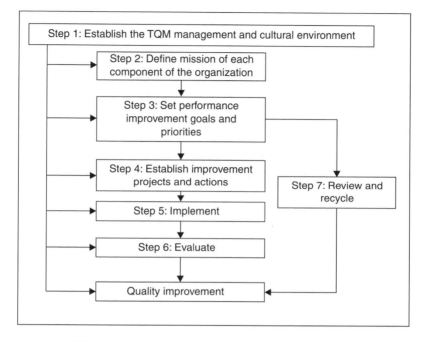

Figure 2.3 TQM model of the Department of Defense (DoD, 1990).

of the 'Quality and Productivity Self-Assessment Guide for Defense Organizations version 1.0' (DoD, 1992). As seen in the figure, the four dimensions are all closely inter-related and the quality climate has profound influence on all other practical aspects. In order to build up a framework suitable for use in the present empirical study, variables constituting these four dimensions have to be identified. A comprehensive literature search is now provided for the purpose.

Summing up the doctrines of three quality gurus namely, Deming (1986), Juran (1951) and Ishikawa (1964), Hackman and Wageman (1995: 312–14) summarized five TQM interventions commonly prescribed by them. Firstly, it is important to know what customers want and what are their requirements and expectations. Therefore, there is a need to explicitly identify and measure data about customer requirements. That is to say, a customer-orientation. Secondly, organizations must select vendors and suppliers based on quality, not price. Thus they must work together to achieve partnerships. Thirdly, as TQM requires the participation of everyone in the organization, teamwork is essential. The gurus advocate the use of cross-functional teams to identify and solve quality problems. The famous quality control circle is one example. Fourthly, as an extension to statistical process control, the use of objective data in minimizing variability is important. Thus scientific methods such as the famous 'seven tools' are used to monitor performance and to identify points of high leverage for performance. Finally, as mentioned earlier, TQM is process-oriented. Thus, process-management heuristics are used to enhance team effectiveness. With these five core elements in mind, we now turn to the writings of other authors.

Goetsch and Davis (1994: 14–18) identified ten key elements in TQM. They are briefly explained here:

1. *Customer focus*: Internal and external customers form the driver for total quality.
2. *Obsession with quality*: The organization must become obsessed with meeting or exceeding the definition of quality.
3. *Scientific approach*: In addition to people's skills, involvement, and empowerment, the scientific approach in structuring work and in decision-making, and problem solving must be adopted.
4. *Long-term commitment*: Total quality management is not just another management innovation which reaps short term results. It is a whole new philosophy.
5. *Teamwork*: The quality company fosters teamwork and partnership with the workforce and their representatives for creating external competitiveness.
6. *Continual improvement systems*: Continual improvement of the system is fundamental to continually improving the quality of products and services.
7. *Education and training*: In a quality organization, everyone is constantly learning.
8. *Freedom through control*: Involving and empowering employees through well-planned and carried out control is fundamental to total quality.
9. *Unity of purpose*: Adversarial management–labor relations are irrelevant when there is unity of purpose for total quality.
10. *Employee involvement and empowerment*: Employee involvement and empowerment increases the likelihood of good decisions and promotes ownership of decisions.

Dale *et al.* (1994: 10–13) identified eight similar key elements of TQM. They are also summarized here:

1. *Commitment and leadership of the chief executive officer*: Top management must take charge personally, provide directions, and exercise forceful leadership.
2. *Planning and organization*: Developing and concretizing a clear and long-term strategy for TQM.
3. *Using tools and techniques*: Enhancing quality awareness in employees by letting employees apply effective problem-solving tools and techniques.
4. *Education and training*: Formal education and training programs should be viewed as an investment in developing the ability and knowledge of employees and helping them realize their potential.
5. *Involvement*: Employees must be viewed as assets which appreciate over time.
6. *Teamwork*: Teamwork is the key feature of involvement and that communication must be effective and widespread.
7. *Measurement and feedback*: Both internal and external indicators must be measured continually for meeting objectives and bridging gaps.
8. *Culture change*: It is necessary to create an organizational culture that is conducive to continuous quality improvement and in which everyone can participate.

Similar key ingredients were suggested by Talley (1991: 31–40) after identifying the common threads of three quality gurus namely, Crosby, Deming, and Juran. They are: (1) management leadership and commitment; (2) strategy; (3) training; (4) participative problem-solving; (5) measurement; (6) statistical process control; (7) continuous company-wide improvement; and (8) customer satisfaction.

Brocka and Brocka (1992: 22–44) also identified eight primary elements of TQM which they call the 'pillars of TQM'. They are: (1) organizational vision; (2) barrier removal; (3) communication; (4) continuous evaluation; (5) continuous improvement; (6) customer–vendor relationships; (7) empowering the worker; and (8) training.

Similarly, Prescott (1995: 22–3) has identified ten essential features of world-class quality organizations. In brief, they are: (1) senior management commitment to total quality; (2) customer-centered strategy; (3) flexible leadership style; (4) supply of qualified, competent, and flexible people; (5) effective utilization of resources; (6) productivity and flexibility are the best of the competition; (7) high customer rating; (8) high employee satisfaction; (9) involvement in community activities; and (10) high investor satisfaction.

Kanji (1994: 106–13) suggested four foundation elements for TQM namely: (1) delight the customers; (2) management by fact; (3) people-based management; and (4) continuous improvement. Each of these principles is translated into practices using two core concepts. To delight the customers, customer satisfaction and internal customers must be emphasized. Management by fact is achieved by applying appropriate internal quality measurement methods and focusing on business process management. People-based management is through teamwork. Managers of an organization must also ensure that everything necessary is in place to allow people to make quality. Finally, continuous improvement emphasizes on prevention and the continuous improvement cycle.

Some common ingredients from the key elements suggested by the various writers on quality are identified and fitted into the four-dimension model described earlier. This constitutes a comprehensive framework of TQM to be used in the present study. It is depicted in Figure 2.4.

ISO 9000 Quality System Certification

It is not easy to measure how successful an organization's quality management is because TQM is clearly more a philosophy than an instrument. Therefore, one usually focuses on whether an organization has achieved some form of internationally recognized award or certification. However, it should be noted that any form of quality award must be made up of criteria which are bound not to perfectly reflect an organization's maturity in TQM. Nevertheless, influential quality awards and certifications such as the Malcom Balridge National Quality Award (MBNQA) in the United States, or the ISO 9000 International Standards for Quality Management are under constant review and revision to accommodate the ever widening arrays of quality concepts. For example, the ISO 9000 family of standards are revised every five years, and the latest revised version commonly known as the ISO 9000: 2000 or the millenium edition was recently published in December 2000.

The Deming Application Prize is probably the earliest award of its type. In commemoration of Deming's contribution to Japan's quality movement, it has been organized by JUSE since 1953 and has been the most prestigious quality award in Japan. Parallel to the Deming Prize in terms of prestige in the United States is the MBNQA created by the US Department of Commerce in 1987. Its award criteria have become a working

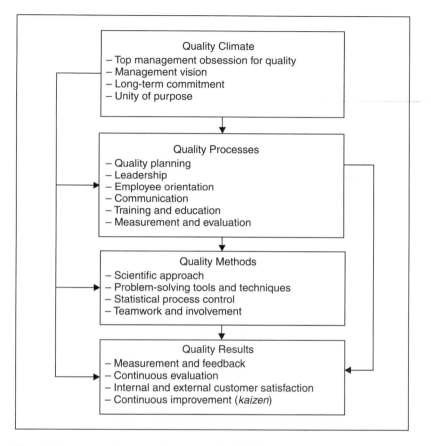

Figure 2.4 A comprehensive framework for TQM.

tool for many organizations (Bounds *et al.*, 1994: 26). The European counterpart for the Deming Prize and the MBNQA is the European Quality Award (EQA). It was introduced in 1992 and was developed by the European Foundation for Quality Management, the European Commission, and the European Organization for Quality (Prescott, 1995: 171–2).

Given the increasing importance of the globalization of business, the need for a set of internationally recognized quality standards has become inevitable. Since the late 1980s, the term ISO 9000 has become a catchword. In 1987, the International Organization for Standardization (ISO), whose membership is now composed of 135 national standards bodies, published the ISO 9000 series of quality management and assurance standards. Today, ISO 9000 is commonly accepted everywhere. Even countries like the United States and Japan which have their own prestigious quality awards cannot bear to ignore it.

According to the ISO, the lack of worldwide compatible standards has led to technical barriers to trade. The purpose of the ISO is to rationalize international trading through the advocacy of world standards. An internationally recognized set of standards can serve as the language of trade in the process of trade liberation of the free-market economies and cross-border investments. Also, global standards are indispensable for accumulating quantitative information leading to the development of new technology. Furthermore, developing countries need standardization for building infrastructures and improving productivity, market competitiveness, and export capability (ISO, 1994b).

Basically, the ISO 9000 is a family of standards for internal quality management as well as external quality assurance purposes (ISO, 1994a). They include ISO 9001 (Quality systems: model for quality assurance in design, development, production, installation, and servicing), ISO 9002 (Quality systems: model for quality assurance in production, installation, and servicing), and ISO 9003 (Quality systems: model for quality assurance in final inspection and testing). Furthermore, the ISO 9004 provides guidance on quality management and quality system elements, but it is not for certification purpose.

In response to the need for a more theory-driven approach to evaluate TQM (e.g. Wilson and Durant, 1994), the latest version ISO 9000: 2000 is designed to center on eight core quality management principles namely: (1) customer focus; (2) leadership; (3) involvement of people; (4) process approach; (5) system approach to management; (6) continual improvement; (7) factual approach to decision-making; and (8) mutually beneficial supplier relationships (ISO, 2001a). Particular emphases have been placed on top management commitment, process approach, and especially continual improvement which was previously pinpointed to be largely ignored (e.g. Kanji, 1998; Curkovic and Pagell, 1999). It can be noticed that these principles are much in line with the core elements described earlier in the framework for TQM. Today, the ISO 9001, ISO 9002, and ISO 9003 standards have been consolidated into one single set of ISO 9000: 2000 Quality Management System Requirement Standards used for certification purpose. On the other hand, ISO 9004: 2000 is the Quality Management System Guidance which is designed to go beyond requirement standards to a more holistic approach to quality management aiming at operational improvement and benefits to all interested parties (ISO, 2001b).

There has been a steady increase of ISO 9000 certifications worldwide. The 1993–94 Mobil survey (ISO 9000 News, January, 1994) revealed that there were at least 70 517 ISO 9000 certificates issued in 76 countries until the end of June 1994, representing an increase of 18 722 certifications as compared to the number in September 1993. Curkovic and Pagell (1999: 51) estimated that there were over 8100 registered sites in the United States by the end of 1995. In Hong Kong, the Hong Kong Quality Assurance Agency had issued until July 1996, 613 certificates (HKQAA, 1996). Furthermore, according to the information provided by the Bureau of Commodity Inspection and Quarantine of the Ministry of Economic Affairs in Taiwan, the number of certificates issued in 1997 had already far passed the 1000 milestone.

At the time of revising the final manuscript of this book, the number of certifications awarded worldwide until December 1999 has already rocketed to at least 343 643 in 150 countries worldwide including 2150 in Hong Kong, 3807 in Taiwan, and 15 109 in mainland China (ISO, 2000). Detailed information can be found in *The ISO Survey of ISO 9000 and ISO 14000 Certificates: Ninth Cycle*, which can be obtained from the ISO homepage (http://www.iso.ch/).

Integrating ISO 9000 with TQM

According to Iizuka (1996: 4–5), ISO 9000 does not assess the organization's results and performance. Rather, it assesses what kind of activities are being managed, and how they are being managed. From the assessment viewpoint, ISO 9000 is conformity assessment, not an award or recognition of an organization's performance. Therefore, it is likely that one may question the usefulness of ISO 9000 relative to the Deming Prize or the MBNQA. In fact, they should be viewed as different but complementary to each other. According to a winner of the MBNQA in the United States, the ISO 9000 standards and the MBNQA criteria are two ends to the same goal. The ISO 9000 can be viewed as the baseline for a company to maintain a good quality system. In other words, ISO 9000 helps to build up a foundation for an organization's TQM activities (Bureau of Business Practice, 1992: 115–17). Nevertheless, Curkovic and Pagell (1999: 55) urged that taking ISO 9000 as a foundation for TQM is a misconception. Since ISO 9000 is not connected directly to product standards, it is possible to have an ISO 9000 system and still manufacture poor quality products. This is true as the ISO has already explicitly stated that 'ISO 9000 is not a product quality label' (ISO, 2000). Therefore, ISO 9000 should be treated as a subset, rather than a foundation, of TQM. According to their study involving 30 companies in four mid-western states in the United States, three main drawbacks of the ISO 9000 were identified. Firstly, companies perceived that getting the ISO 9000 requires tremendous amount of paperwork. Thus it is only a paper-driven process. Secondly, ISO 9000 does nothing to ensure continuous improvement (note the response of the latest ISO 9000: 2000 to this). Thirdly, the certification process requires high costs and provides little pay-off. Despite such criticisms, the authors argued that according to their findings, companies which are willing to invest time and energy into the process can reap significant rewards. It is a matter of possessing the right attitude to it. Companies which take advantage of ISO 9000 will benefit while those which view it as a nuisance will be missing out a golden opportunity (Curkovic and Pagell, 1999: 65).

Curkovic and Handfield (1996) presented a host of items not covered by the ISO 9000 standards. Similarly, Kanji (1998) pointed out that important TQM principles such as delighting the customer and continuous improvement are not an integral part of ISO 9000 (again note the response of ISO 9000: 2000 to this). Also, assuring quality by using one standard only for different types of industries is only a general and vague approach. ISO 9000 itself does not guarantee that one's product or service is of high quality or free from defect. Therefore he proposed a framework for process innovation in order to enhance the effectiveness of ISO 9000 and its relationship with TQM principles. Under this framework, process innovation is based on three aspects namely: (1) process definition; (2) process improvement; and (3) process management. In integrating process definition with ISO 9000, one must first define suitable processes under which the ISO standards are to be implemented. The primary role here is to build the foundation for continuous improvement of ISO 9000. Then the defined processes must be geared on a set of goals for process improvement. Benchmarking can be used here to help identify factors which should be incorporated in the process improvement. Finally, the requirement clauses of ISO 9001 can be divided into three main areas for process management namely: (1) organization and quality system; (2) customers; and (3) design, product and services. Thus, if an organization incorporates these three types of process management with ISO 9000, a reasonable first step towards TQM can be achieved. Moreover, Kanji also suggested that self-assessment of an organization's TQM process over time should be integrated with the internal auditing requirement of ISO 9000, hence using the ISO standards to build up a foundation for continuous process improvement.

Iizuka (1996: 13–20) also provided some insights as to integrating ISO 9000 with TQM. Firstly, external quality assurance by third party assessment in ISO 9000 has not been specified in TQM. It provides a valuable experience and challenge for the organization engaging in TQM. Secondly, ISO 9000 can be used to enhance TQM primarily through external pressures demanding continual quality system review. In the beginning, an organization may have applied for ISO 9000 registration simply because of customer demand. Later on, the organization should see that adopting ISO 9000 is helpful in invigorating its internal quality management system.

Another point suggested by Iizuka is of particular importance to Japan. However, organizations in other nations can also take this as a reference. He pointed out that the independence of management functions such as planning, implementation, and verification, characterized by ISO 9000 was not viewed as imperative in Japanese-style management. Following ISO 9000 allows Japanese companies to experiment and accommodate management systems different from theirs. This is in line with the proposal of the Japan Productivity Center for Socio-Economic Development to redesign the Japanese management systems and practices (Japan Productivity Center or Socio-Economic Development, 1994; Miyai, 1995). The ISO 9000 can also open a path to TQM. As Iizuka has argued, after undergoing external quality audit three or four times, a number of companies which have obtained ISO 9000 registration reported that they wished to be evaluated by quality standards much higher than those under ISO 9000. In other words, they feel the need to embark on the TQM journey.

The benefits of implementing ISO 9000

As ISO 9000 essentially aims at improving the quality management system of an organization, appropriate implementation of ISO 9000 is often believed to help the organization enhance its internal operations. According to a survey conducted by Lee (1994), ISO 9000 mostly helps intrinsically in uplifting team spirit and reducing employee conflicts. Extrinsic benefits such as improvement of business performance was however not so highly acknowledged. This is not difficult to understand because ISO 9000 is only a first step in TQM which represents a long-term endeavor. Substantial extrinsic impacts can be reaped only if the company continues to embark on TQM after the ISO certification. According to the survey, over 70 per cent of the sampled companies expressed that they would engage in TQM. Although the sample size of this survey was obviously insufficient for generalization (19 service companies and 16 manufacturing companies), it nevertheless has provided some insights.

The survey also illustrated some practical aspects of implementing ISO 9000. For example, ISO 9000 is applicable to any industry and can be obtained by companies of any size. Curkovic and Pagell (1999) reported in their survey of American firms that the cost of obtaining ISO 9000 and the paper-driven process are major preoccupations of companies wishing to undergo the certification process. However, Lee (1994) concluded that the cost of implementing ISO 9000 is not too high actually, and it is often not necessary to increase manpower in order to cope with the certification process.

In a subsequent study by the same author using a larger number of sampled companies in 1996 (Lee, 1998), it was consistently found that the most acknowledged benefits of implementing ISO 9000 were still the enhancement of team spirit and the reduction of staff conflict. The importance of ISO 9000 as a good starting point for engaging in the TQM journey is nonetheless justified. The consistent implementation of ISO 9000 through its standardization of quality systems can eventually help an organization gain competitive advantage in the international marketplace (Curkovic and Pagell, 1999: 65).

Impact of TQM on organizational performance

Some insights as to the impact of TQM activities on organizational performance are given in this section. A number of commonly found difficulties in and misconceptions about the implementation of TQM are also provided.

Extrinsic impacts of TQM

It is possible to classify the impacts and benefits of implementing TQM into two main types namely, extrinsic and intrinsic. Extrinsic benefits are commonly known in the form of real economic benefits such as the reduction of costs and lead time and the increase in product profitability and market share. Hansen (1994) pointed out that the main economic benefit of TQM is the increase of the gain/cost ratio. Gains are increased mainly through the marketing of new products and services as well as the improvement of existing products and services. Specifically, the improvement of products and services, the reduction of time to market, the gaining of new customers and the retaining of existing customers, the exploitation of reputation, and the improvement of facility utilization are commonly acknowledged. On the other hand, costs of various kinds can be reduced.

Reviewing what the quality gurus have said is important in understanding the basics of such economic benefits. In 1950, Deming pointed out a chain reaction model involving quality, productivity, lower costs, and market captivation during his lectures in Japan. According to him, the improvement of quality leads to decreased cost due to less rework, fewer mistakes, delays, snags, and better use of machine time and materials. This in turn leads to improved productivity, followed by the captivation of the market with better quality and lower prices. The organization is thus able to stay in business and to provide more and more job opportunities (Deming, 1986: 3).

Economic benefits brought by TQM can also be appreciated through the concept of 'cost of quality' firstly proposed by Feigenbaum and later refined by Juran. The two basic components of the concept are the cost of conformance and the cost of non-conformance. The former includes prevention costs (e.g. cost of quality planning) and appraisal costs (e.g. material inspection and quality audit costs). The latter includes internal failure costs (e.g. rework and trouble-shooting or fire-fighting) and external failure costs (e.g. costs of goods returned and lost market share). Juran believed that a sound quality management system can reduce all of the above costs. He also pointed out that in the beginning of any quality journey such costs may increase spontaneously as sporadic spikes. However, in the long run, all the costs can be minimized (Juran, 1988, 1989, 1992).

Feigenbaum also suggested an even wider scope of extrinsic benefits. For example, he argued that the costs of quality and safety today account for an increasingly significant proportion of the gross national product. Product and service quality is fundamental to business health, growth, and economic viability (Feigenbaum, 1991: 5). Taguchi's (1986) 'loss to society' concept can be seen parallel to Feigenbaum's suggestion.

Intrinsic impacts of TQM

Kano (1994: 44) suggested two fundamental impacts of TQM. Firstly, the creation of product and service quality which aims to contribute to others. Secondly, the improvement of employees' and workers' quality of work life. As TQM is everybody's job, a quality work life, allowing employee and worker participation, helps to uplift sense of belonging and motivation. As reported by Hackman and Wageman (1995: 317), most TQM organizations create employee suggestion systems and have quality meetings between managers and employees. The aspiration to involve everyone in quality is reinforced through the celebrations of quality-related events.

Among a dozen of methods to enhance employee involvement, the most popular is probably the quality control circle (QCC). Quality control circles have their root in Japan since 1962 (Ishikawa, 1985: 152). In 1970, the QCC Headquarters in Japan published a booklet entitled *QC circle koryo* (English edition published in 1980 as *General Principles of the QC Circle*) and defined a QCC as 'a small group to perform voluntarily quality control activities within the same workshop. This small group carries on continuously, as part of company-wide quality control activity, self and mutual improvement and control and improvement within the workshop utilizing quality control techniques, with all members participating' (QC Circle Headquarters, JUSE, 1980: 1). Today, the use of QCCs in organizations engaging in quality is common worldwide. Ishikawa cited ten useful guides in conducting successful QCC activities namely: (1) self-development; (2) voluntarism; (3) group activity; (4) participation by all employees; (5) utilization of QC techniques; (6) activities closely connected with the workplace; (7) vitality and continuity in QC activities; (8) mutual development; (9) originality and creativity; and (10) awareness of quality, problems, and improvement (Ishikawa, 1985: 140–3).

In an empirical study of quality motivation by Cheng and Chan (1999: 972–3), the authors identified two main quality motivators. The first factor principally focused on the improvement of work efficiency, effectiveness, and reducing scrap and rework in the production process and hence the benefits to the company. This factor was named the 'technological' dimension of quality motivation. The second factor was mainly concerned with personal career development and the enhancement of interpersonal relationships and was named the 'humanistic' dimension of quality motivation. Cheng and Chan's empirical study and Lee's surveys on the impact of ISO 9000 described earlier have both appropriately pointed out the use of TQM or ISO 9000 to create both extrinsic and intrinsic or behavioral outcomes.

In fact, it is possible to juxtapose these findings with two earlier behavioral models of TQM emphasizing on the hard and soft outcomes of introducing QCCs. These are Kido's (1986) and Nita's (1978) QCC models which are based on familiar organizational behavior theories looking into processes and outcomes. As reported by Onglatco (1988: 36), Kido's conceptual model specifies that small group activities yield first-level outcomes such as increased participation in decisions, strengthening of group functions, changes in work content, and promotion of developmental activities. These lead to second-level outcomes, such as enhanced volition, goal clarity and centralization, and acquisition of skills and knowledge. These outcomes in turn lead to final effects, in terms of hard and soft outcomes. Hard outcomes are in the forms of reducing costs and defective rates and increase in safety and operation rates. Soft outcomes include social, work, and growth satisfaction. Nita's conceptual model of circle activity effects is at a more macro level as compared to Kido's. Circle activity effects are divided into direct improvement outcomes and indirect organizational outcomes. The former refer to better product and service quality, cost reduction, and other tangible outcomes which the activity yields in the form of long- or short-term economic benefits to the organization. Indirect outcomes, on the other hand, refer to outcomes that arise from undertaking the activity process itself, like for example, improved communication in the workplace (Onglatco, 1988: 36–7). It can be seen that apart from extrinsic benefits, TQM activities mainly enhance the psychological factor so that group members feel a sense of belonging and fulfillment.

Total quality management recognizes that people are motivated by something more than economic benefits. The old economic model of the firm which only focuses on profit maximization and personal goal satisfaction must be abandoned. The new TQM paradigm envisages a convergence of the long-term interests of employees, shareholders, customers, and stakeholders. By improving quality, the organization creates a secure future for itself and its employees. In line with the transcendent view of quality, quality is a form of perfection that has intrinsic value. A quality product is a work of art in the sense that it embodies the human quest for perfection. Therefore, TQM represents a return to the values of craftsmanship that have fallen victim to twentieth century management methods (Grant *et al.*, 1994: 31).

Difficulties and misconceptions about TQM

As stated repeatedly, TQM is a philosophy rather than a management technique or tool. Therefore, the maturity of TQM leading to success in any organization is a long-term endeavor. It can easily take up to ten years to put the fundamental principles, procedures, and systems of TQM into place (Lascelles and Dale, 1994: 316). Failures are typically reflections of misunderstandings about the central philosophy of TQM.

According to a research (Dale, 1991) on the difficulties faced by organizations in their quality improvement efforts, organizations found difficulties both in introducing and sustaining TQM activities. In particular, the lack of top management commitment and vision and a 'flavor of the month' type attitude are significant obstacles to introducing TQM. Furthermore, pressures and constraints in terms of time, workload, and resources, and the lack of continuous commitment are the main inhibitors to sustaining TQM. Kanji (1996), using a real life case of a medium-sized service company, vividly illustrated 12 main pitfalls which affected the company's TQM implementation. All the problems actually started with the managing director, confirming that top management commitment and leadership are the most important of all. The dozen of problems include: (1) lack of constancy of purpose; (2) failure to adopt a new philosophy; (3) failure to institute change in the organization; (4) refusal to provide industry-recognized training to the workforce; (5) management by fear and intimidation; (6) barriers among departments; (7) lack of a learning culture; (8) unrealistic overwork; (9) failure to make decisions based on objective evidence; (10) not taking a company-wide scope of quality improvement; (11) putting teamwork to second importance; and (12) policies created in secret (p. 342).

To round up, four main barriers as reported by Lascelles and Dale (1994) can summarize the main pitfalls of implementing TQM.

1. *The nature of management leadership*: The leadership style of many top managers is often transactional rather than transformational (Lascelles and Dale, 1994: 320). That is to say, they merely react to events rather than shape future events. This is obviously in contrast with the main principle of TQM which emphasizes on integrating quality into design through well sought out quality planning. This traditional way of management results in many lost opportunities due to trouble-shooting or fire-fighting. To be successful in TQM, managers have to shift their management focus from the traditional to a new paradigm.

2. *Fear of change*: Changing from the traditional to a new paradigm requires substantial effort. Change consists of two elements, namely, the intended change and the social consequence of the intended change. The social consequence becomes a trouble when there is a clash between the culture of the change advocates and that of the recipients (Juran, 1992: 430). Juran thus recommended some rules to deal with cultural resistance. For example, the recipient society should be provided with participation and enough time to accommodate changes. Any change should start on a small scale and should be kept flexible. A favorable social climate should be created by top management through setting themselves as good examples. Any change should be woven into the existing and acceptable part of the cultural pattern. Problems raised by the recipient society should

be treated positively and constructively. That is to say, people must be treated with dignity and trust (pp. 433–4).

3. *Inadequate skills and resources to facilitate improvement*: This relates mainly to how and what kind of training is being deployed to the organizational members. For example, lack of emphasis on inter-departmental and cross-functional skills, over-reliance on training packages provided by consultants, and the launching of too many quality improvement initiatives at the same time making things difficult to manage (Dale and Boaden, 1994) should be avoided. Ishikawa (1985: 141) had appropriately addressed the problem on training. He stated that technical training alone is not enough. As TQM is a philosophy rather than a technique, training must be accompanied by education.

4. *A lack of information to support the improvement process*: The effective-ness of the quality improvement process is dependent on the availability of relevant, reliable, and objective information and the communication methods used (Lascelles and Dale, 1994: 327). Organizations wishing to obtain ISO 9000 certifications should pay particular attention to this point. For example, document and data control and the control of quality records are specific requirements of ISO 9001. Total quality management itself is essentially a philo-sophy. However, the concretization of the philosophy is largely based on scientific methods of management. Price (1984: 328) appropriately suggested three rules namely, no measurement without recording, no recording without analysis, and no analysis without action.

The chapter has concluded as a comprehensive literature review on quality, TQM, and ISO 9000. Chapter 3 will review values and culture as the second major ingredient in the present empirical study.

3
Value, Culture, and Chinese Cultural Values

In this chapter, culture as the second major ingredient of the present empirical research is reviewed. Representative definitions of values and culture are given and discussed. Then, the particularities of Chinese cultural values are presented.

Defining value

The concept of value-orientation (Kluckhohn and Strodtbeck, 1961) is commonly used in cross-cultural management studies (Negandhi, 1986). It stems from the original definition of value by Kluckhohn (1951: 395) whereby 'a value is a conception, explicit or implicit, distinctive of an individual or a group, of the desirable which influences the selection from available modes, means, and ends of actions'. Several other representative definitions of value are compared here. For example, Parsons (1951: 12) defined a value as 'an element of a shared symbolic system which serves as a criterion or standard for selection among the alternatives of orientation which are intrinsically open in a situation'. Rokeach (1973: 159–60) defined a person having a value as 'having an enduring belief that a specific mode of conduct or end-state of existence is personally and socially preferable to alternative modes of conduct or end-states of existence'. Hofstede (1980: 19) defined a value as 'a broad tendency to prefer certain states of affairs over others'. Finally, Yang (1986: 115) defined it as 'the core component of a class of generalized attitudes concerning what is desirable or undesirable, which directs behavior on a long-term basis towards some goals in preference to others'. Several common points can be highlighted.

1. There is a degree of awareness or a continuum of implicitness or explicitness (Kluckhohn and Strodtbeck, 1961: 5). As argued by Bem (1970: 16), values can be either non-consciously taken for granted or taken as a direct derivation from experience or some external authority.
2. There is a motivational and evaluative element expressed as an orientation to the improvement of a gratification–deprivation balance of the actor (Parsons, 1951: 12). Parsons' (1951) motivational orientation of the actor includes the cognitive, the cathectic, and the evaluative aspects. Kluckhohn and Strodtbeck (1961) included similar cognitive, affective, and directive aspects in the transactional process. Thus values influence behaviors and actions.
3. In line with the point mentioned above, there is a desired versus desirable dichotomy. Hofstede (1980) warned that the two should not be equated in order to avoid positivistic fallacy (Levitine, 1973) even though behaviors or actions are influenced by values.
4. There is also a time orientation so that a value is described as enduring or sticky. Hofstede (1980) described this characteristic as a mental program while Rokeach (1973) differentiated between terminal values and instrumental values.
5. The values held by a person collectively form a 'value system' or 'value hierarchy'. Though hierarchical in nature, a person may simultaneously hold different and even conflicting values (Hofstede, 1980: 19). Also, each value possesses both 'intensity' and 'direction' (p. 20), or 'intensity' and 'modality' (Kluckhohn, 1951: 413–14).

In order to compare values cross-culturally, it is necessary to examine the value-orientations of each culture. Kluckhohn and Strodtbeck's value orientation concept was built upon three assumptions. Firstly, 'there is a limited number of common human problems for which all peoples at all times must find some solutions'. Secondly, 'while there is variability in solutions of all problems, it is neither limitless nor random but is definitely variable within a range of possible solutions'. Thirdly, and most important of all, 'all alternatives of all solutions are present in all societies at all times but are differentially preferred' (Kluckhohn and Strodtbeck, 1961: 10). Thus, five questions have been singled out in particular to observe the total range of variations in five orientations. They include: (1) Human nature orientation: what is the character of innate human nature? (2) Man-nature orientation: what is the relation of man to nature and super-nature? (3) Time orientation: what is the temporal focus of human life? (4) Activity orientation: what is the modality of human activity? (5) Relational orientation: what is the modality of man's relationship to other men? (p. 11).

Defining culture

Grounded on Kluckhohn's definition of values, and concluding their review of various definitions found in the anthropological literature, Kroeber and Kluckhohn defined a culture as 'consisting of patterns, explicit and implicit, of and for behaviors (ways of thinking, feeling, and reacting) acquired and transmitted mainly by symbols including embodiments in artifacts, traditional (historically derived and selected) ideas and especially their attached values; cultural systems may be considered as products of actions and as conditioning elements of future actions' (Kroeber and Kluckhohn, 1952: 181; Kluckhohn, 1951: 86).

Two important points concerning culture should be noted here. Firstly, values are among the building blocks of culture (Hofstede, 1980: 25). Parsons, in his study of action systems, pointed out that value-orientation is the logical device for articulating cultural traditions into an action system (Parsons, 1951: 12). Thus, culture is the result of value systems, and behaviors and actions are influenced by culture. Secondly, culture has a collective sense. As argued by Parsons again, culture is 'transmitted', 'learned', and 'shared' (Parsons, 1951: 15). Thus, Hofstede, in simple, treated culture as 'the collective programming of the mind which distinguishes the members of one human group from another' (Hofstede, 1980: 25). From these explanations, it can be understood that although no single individual will possess all the cultural characteristics of the group to which one belongs, culture is a concept resting on the human collectivity level. Furthermore, the 'super-organic' concept of Kroeber (1917) is of fundamental importance to the theoretical assumptions of culture. He argued that culture is super-organic, above and beyond its biological and psychological bases, having an independent existence at its own level. It remains relatively stable and unchanged irrespective of a large turnover in membership within each new generation.

It is also possible to delineate the cultural patterns of different societies, nations, and groups by identifying the dimensions of cultures through analyzing the different combinations of value orientations (Kluckhohn and Strodtbeck, 1961). Parsons' famous 'pattern variables' offer to achieve this objective (Parsons, 1951: 67; Words in parentheses from Hofstede, 1980: 45–6):

1. *The gratification–discipline dilemma*: affectivity (need gratification) versus affective neutrality (restrain of impulses);

2. *The private–collective interest dilemma*: self-orientation versus collect-ivity-orientation;
3. *The choice between types of value orientation standards*: universalism (applying general standards) versus particularism (taking particular relationships into account);
4. *The choice between modalities of the social object*: achievement (judging others by what they do) versus ascription (judging others by who they are); and
5. *The definition of scope of interest in the object*: specificity (limiting relations to others to specific spheres) versus diffuseness (no prior limitations to nature of relations).

It is important here to clarify some issues on the different levels of analysis in cultural studies. First of all, it has been reassured from the above discussions that values or value systems are part of a culture and that culture is understood in the collective sense. Hofstede pointed out that the study of culture and personality, often termed 'psychological anthropology', is based on two different levels of analysis. The study of culture pertains to a human collectivity, while the study of personality pertains to an individual. Based on Guilford's (1959) definition of personality (the interactive aggregate of personal characteristics that influence the individual's response to environment), he defined culture as 'the interactive aggregate of common characteristics that influence a human group's response to its environment' (Hofstede, 1980: 25). Similarly, Inkeles and Levinson (1954: 988) argued that concepts such as Kluckhohn's value orientation refer to patterning in the culture rather than in the individual personality.

In other words, it is possible to have two inter-related levels of analysis. As pointed out by Bond, analyses in the study of values can be conducted based on the individual level and the cultural level. Although people often speak of individuals holding values, not of coun-tries holding values, it is possible to characterize the values of a country through averaging the scores given to a set of values by a representative sample of persons from that country (Bond, 1996: 211). Several import-ant studies are based on the cultural level in this way. For example, Hofstede's (1980) mammoth project and many of its continuations, the Chinese value survey (The Chinese Culture Connection, 1987), and the Schwartz value survey (Schwartz and Bilsky, 1987, 1990). Interestingly, Bond pointed out that individual-level studies of values can also be performed based on findings from cultural-level studies of values. For example, in Bond (1988), he presented the individual-level analysis of the data collected by the Chinese Cultural Connection.

Chinese cultural values in relation to Confucian teachings based on the value orientation framework

There have been a number of studies on Chinese cultural values based on an evaluative–attitudinal approach during the past decades. Most of the studies agree with the classical eco-cultural model (Berry *et al.*, 1992), in which culture is a result of the social system, which is itself characterized by the subsistence system (e.g. agricultural, gathering, fishing, pastoral, or hunting) influenced by the ecological environment as well as the genetic traits of the race. For example, Yang (1986: 162) provided a simplified cultural-ecological view of the Chinese culture. He argued that the Chinese agricultural system has led to a social structure emphasizing hierarchical organization, collectivistic functioning, generalized familization, structural tightness, and social homogeneity. Furthermore, dominant moral and religious thoughts or doctrines such as Confucianism, Taoism, and Buddhism helped shape the Chinese character. These have led to a social-oriented character of the Chinese as exemplified in the collectivistic, other, and relationship orientations as well as the submissive, inhibited, and effeminate dispositions.

Such characteristics are consistent with the traditional cultural pattern of the Chinese as described by Parsons. For example, based on different combinations of his pattern variables, he pointed out that the traditional Chinese value of collectivism is a result of underscoring collective achievements and responsibilities towards collectivities (Parsons, 1951: 96). A combination of particularism and achievement emphasizes on a harmonious order to maintain or restore men's responsibilities (p. 111). Also, the classical Chinese social structure is organized primarily based on kinship but sometimes extending beyond the conjugal family. It is characterized by the continuity with ancestors, hierarchical relationships, and a general orientation to collective morality. Responsibilities, ranging from the Emperor's responsibility for the society to the father's responsibility for his family, emphasize the functioning of collectivities (p. 195). The close connection between responsibility and superiority of status characterized the Chinese system to be both collectivistic and authoritarian. Individualistically oriented achievements are supressed due to the weakness of universalism (p. 197).

Yau (1994) attempted to classify typical Chinese cultural values according to the value orientation framework and obtained a number

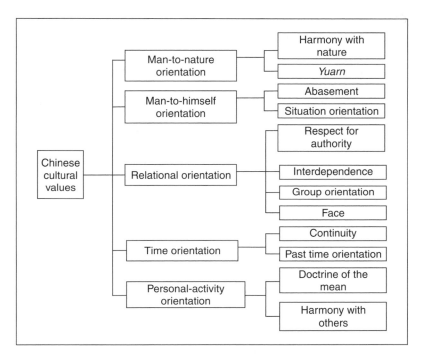

Figure 3.1 Classification of Chinese cultural values (Yau, 1994: 68).

of specific values as shown in Figure 3.1. Each of the Chinese cultural values is briefly explained with examples drawn mainly from the teachings of Confucius and some empirical studies on Chinese psychology.

Harmony with nature

Based on the eco-cultural model (Berry *et al.*, 1992), the ancient Chinese who were primarily peasants watched closely the transformations of nature, in particular the operations of the four seasons which regulated their farming activities. They gradually developed a belief that natural phenomena were closely related to human affairs (Lu, 1983: 45–6, 48). Confucius' essential doctrine of 'oneness (harmony and union) between Heaven and man' is likely to be derived from this eco-cultural property. In his *Doctrine of the Mean*, it contained the following passage:

> What Heaven/Nature (*Tian*) imparts to man is called human nature. To follow our nature is called the Way (*Tao*). Cultivating the Way is called education.

The Chinese believe that nature has the 'Way' (*Tao*). They regard man as a part of nature, and believe that man should not try to overcome or master nature but has to learn how to adapt for harmony (Yau, 1994: 69). This is parallel to Weber's descriptions of 'adaptation to the world' but not 'mastery over the world' (Parsons, 1951: 111). As Morris and Jones (1955: 527) revealed their findings in their 'Ways to Live' survey, Chinese respondents ranked the highest preference rating for way number 13 namely, 'Obey the cosmic purposes'. Yang (1986) later pointed out that due to a mistake in translation, Way 13 was thus rated so high by the Chinese sample. Nevertheless, he also argued that such a high rating cannot be completely attributed to the translation error and the Chinese had fairly good reasons to prefer Way 13 (p. 118).

However, it is not to say that the Chinese are so fatalistic and pessimistic that they do not actively pursue a desirable life or that they do not resent on things lost in life. Instead, they believe that misfortunes in life are to be followed by luck in the future or even in the next life as the Chinese saying goes: 'Man has three misfortunes and six fortunes in life'. This is only when the Way is followed and harmony with nature maintained. The following quote from *The Analects* is clear about the point.

> You Zi said, 'In practicing the rules of propriety, it is harmony that is prized. This is what is so precious in the ways of the ancient kings. They followed this principle in things small and great. Yet it is not to be observed in all cases. To know how such harmony should be prized, yet manifest it without regulating it by the rules of propriety, is something which should not be done.'
>
> (The Analects, 1, 12)

The Chinese put a lot of emphasis on morality and man has to be responsible for maintaining the given social structure as a going concern. This can be seen reflected in the teachings of Confucius in *The Analects*. For example,

> The Master said, 'Wealth and rank are what every man desires, but if they cannot be obtained except at the expense of the Way, he does not accept them. Poverty and low station are what every man detests, but if it can only be done at the expense of the Way, avoiding them is not for him. The nobleman who departs from humanity – how can he be worthy of the name of noble man? Never for a moment does the noble man forswear his humanity. Never is he so

harried that he does not cleave to this, never so endangered that he does not cleave to this.'

(The Analects, 4, 5)

Yuarn

Yuarn, the predetermination of relationships with things or people in life by a super-natural force too sophisticated for the ordinary man to understand, stems from the concept of *Karma* in Buddhism. Yau (1994: 69) pointed out that after almost two thousand years of assimilation, its meaning has deviated from its original. He mentioned that *yuarn* has two senses. Firstly, as things in life such as friendship and marriage are dependent upon *yuarn*, it leads to tragic consequences when such relationships cease. Secondly, *yuarn* has a positive sense in that it leads to the development of self-reliance so that people actively seek for *yuarn* (p. 70). For example, Lee (1985) noted how one can accumulate *yuarnfen* (predestined affinity) through behaviors in life, and it is important to involve oneself in relationships and search out a suitable partner (Goodwin and Tang, 1996: 297).

Cheung explained the concept of *yuarn* from another point of view based on the attribution process in psychopathology. She argued that *yuarn* acts as an important external attribution for success or failure in interpersonal relationships among the Chinese. It helps to maintain interpersonal harmony by attributing the success or failure of relationships to forces beyond one's personal control, thus protecting one's face and saving the face of others (Cheung, 1996: 201–2). Similarly, Yang and Ho (1988) argued that a successful individual tends to ascribe his or her success to the intervention of a significant other, the maintenance of good social relations, collective efforts, and *yuarn*. On the other hand, *yuarn* was found to be an attribution to failures (Yu, 1996: 243–4). *Yuarn* was also believed to be one explanation of why the Chinese report less positive self-concept than other Westerners who frequently report a pattern of ego-defensive attributions (Leung, 1996: 256). Drawing from studies conducted in Taiwan and Hong Kong (Yang and Ho, 1988; Huang *et al.*, 1983), Crittenden (1996: 266) stated that the idea of *yuarn* remains alive in the modern Chinese culture, but with a lessened religious connotation than in the past.

Abasement

The Chinese see abasement as an expression of modesty, humbleness, and politeness. Modesty and self-effacement are two important virtues that a child or a subordinate uses to cultivate the mind (Yau, 1994: 71). As pointed out by Cheng (1990: 182–3), propriety, humility, and sincerity are the moral aims of Confucian teachings.

Singh *et al.* (1962), on applying the Edwards personal preference schedule to student samples in America, China, and India, found that the Chinese scored relatively high on the abasement scale. A plausible reason for this phenomenon lies in the central doctrine of Confucius, the so-called 'Five Cardinal Relations (*Wu Lun*)'. They refer to the hierarchical relationships between sovereign and subject, father and son, elder brother and younger brother, husband and wife, and friend and friend. In each case, the senior member is accorded a wide range of prerogatives and authority with respect to the junior (Bond and Hwang, 1986: 215). Thus in the past, a Chinese would address oneself as 'the unworthy' and 'the unfilial' in front of the teacher and the parent respectively (Yau, 1994: 71). Although such names are no more common today (though they still exist sometimes in formal writings), the sense of respect for higher authority still prevails. This can be seen reflected in Hofstede's (1980) finding concerning the large power distance found in Chinese societies. Nevertheless, even Confucius himself, so renowned as a sage, was so humble to say:

> The *sheng* (sage) and *jen* (love); how dare I rank myself with them?
>
> (The Analects, 7, 23)

Situation orientation

Yau (1994: 71) claimed that the situation-oriented and pragmatic characteristic of the Chinese is a result of their child-rearing practices in which a child is taught not only by the parents, but also by a host of extended or joint family members (e.g. paternal and maternal grandparents, uncles and aunts, cousins, and others), so that the child is exposed to many different points of view. This appears to be a natural consequence as the traditional Chinese is used to cohabitation with more than one generation of family members, as the popular Chinese saying 'Three generations in a house' goes.

Comparatively speaking, the Chinese appear to be less dogmatic and tend to be more flexible in following a learned principle. Yang (1986), in his discussion of the temperamental characteristics of Chinese personality, pointed out that the Chinese have been characterized as valuing common sense and utilitarian ways of thinking highly. Drawing from the empirical studies conducted by Hellersberg

(1953) and Sue and Kirk (1972), he concluded that the common international image of the Chinese as practical-minded people is supported.

The practical-mindedness or realism of the Chinese also gives rise to a positive and committed attitude. Lu (1983) mentioned about the Chinese cultural characteristic of 'this-worldliness'. He pointed out that the Confucianists do recognize spiritual beings in the form of *yang* and *yin* (positive and negative spiritual forces). However, these spiritual beings would never be allowed to interfere with human activities. Thus, for a Confucianist, immortality of race and culture rather than the soul is what one strives for.

This explains why the Chinese are 'this-worldly'; why they are concerned with the cultivation of one's virtue in order not to shame their ancestors and to pass on their descendants something which they may be proud of; and why they esteem scholarship. He quoted from Lin (1935: 401) the following description of the Chinese pagan: 'one who starts out with this earthy life as all we can or need to bother about, wishes to live intently and happily as long as his life lasts'.

Respect for authority

This cultural value is largely built upon the 'Five Cardinal Relations' mentioned above. The mechanism of the relations is based on Confucius' teaching on the rules of proper behavior or propriety (*li*) so that rights and responsibilities for each are entailed. Harmony is realized if each member of the unit was conscientious in following the requirements of his or her role (Bond and Hwang, 1986: 215). Confucius' teachings have especially emphasized on respect for sovereignty, respect for teachers, and filial piety. Some quotes from Confucius are given as examples.

I imitate, follow, and observe the virtue of King Wen, And daily there is tranquillity in all the regions

(The Book of Poetry, 4, 1, ode 7)

Take your pattern from King Wen, And the myriad states will repose confidence in you

(The Book of Poetry, 3, 1, ode 1, 7)

There are three essentials in our lives, and they should be regarded as the same in importance: parents who beget us, teachers who teach us, and the kings who feed us.

(The Narratives of the States, *Chin Yu*)

The Master said, 'Those who love their parents dare not show hatred to others. Those who respect their parents, dare not show rudeness to others.

(The Book of Filial Piety, *T'ien Tzu*)

Filial piety is the root of virtue, and the origin of culture . . . To establish oneself and walk according to the right way (*Tao*), in order to glorify one's parents: this is the culmination of filial piety. Filial piety begins with serving one's parents, leading to serving one's king, and ends in establishing oneself . . .

(The Book of Filial Piety, *K'ai Tsung Ming I*)

Bond and Hwang (1986: 216) pointed out that there is a potential danger involving such a considerable inequality of power since abuse of one's superior position can put the opposite party in serious jeopardy. Nevertheless, Yang described that the highly authoritarian attitudes of the Chinese can be inferred from their extremely strong sense of filial piety. One main component of authoritarianism is the unconditional submissiveness to authority. Drawing from studies by Chu (1967), Hiniker (1969), and Yang (1970), he reported that the Chinese are rather skillful in showing deference towards whomever they consider an authority. The best policy is always to behave like a subordinate and to treat the other as an authority, unless the person clearly knows that he himself is the authority in the relationship (Yang, 1986: 127–8). This is obviously a result of combining the values of abasement and respect for authority together.

Interdependence

Confucius once said, 'All within the four seas are brothers' (The Analects, 12, 5, 4). Weber (1951) stated that the Chinese depend enormously on particularistic type of trust which intentionally leave people in their personal relations as naturally grown. According to Wong (1991: 13–25), there is a high level of system as well as personal trust in Hong Kong and this could explain to a certain extent the business success of Chinese entrepreneurs in Hong Kong and the overseas Chinese communities.

Yau pointed out two elements which are important to the Chinese in terms of interpersonal relations. There are also logical reasons to believe that these two elements serve to enhance personal and system trust. The first element is the principle of 'doing favors' (*renqing*). Favors done for others are often considered as social investments for which returns are expected (Yau, 1994: 73). The reciprocal exchange of favors serves as a lubricant in the Chinese way of doing business. However, the concept of '*renqing*' should not be thought to be too instrumental. In Chinese society, when one has either happy occasions or difficulties, his or her acquaintances are expected to offer a gift or render some substantial assistance (Gabrenya and Hwang, 1996: 313–14). This in fact represents a way of proper conduct, propriety (*li*), and love (*jen*).

The other important element is 'face' (*lien* and *mien-tsu*). Hu (1944: 45) defined '*lien*' as something that 'represents the confidence of society in the integrity of ego's moral character, the loss of which makes it impossible for him or her to function properly within the community' and '*mien-tsu*' as 'a reputation achieved through getting on in life, through success and ostentation'. Face management is essential in maintaining the existing role relationships and preserving interpersonal harmony (Gao *et al.*, 1996: 289). In Chinese society, saying someone 'doesn't want face' (*bu yao lien*) is a great insult to the person's moral character meaning that he or she is nasty, shameless, and immoral. However, saying someone 'has no face' (*mei you mien-tsu*) simply means that he or she does not deserve honor or glory (Gabrenya and Hwang, 1996: 313). Confucius' teaching on propriety has put particular emphases on the principle of forgiveness (*shudao*) as he once said, 'Do not to others what you would not want done to yourself' (The Analects, 15, 23; The Doctrine of the Mean, 13, 3). The most common practice of this principle of forgiveness is by avoiding to hurt another's face in social interactions (Gabrenya and Hwang, 1996: 313).

'The mountain and the water will meet some day'. This very popular Chinese saying best demonstrates the emphasis on interdependence and trust. The Chinese, probably due to their belief in *yuarn*, strongly believe that people and even enemies will meet some day and may need each other's assistance. In order to avoid any potential conflict and embarrassment, it is best to treat each other with propriety and not to go too far (the doctrine of the mean) as illustrated in the following saying of Confucius:

> The man of love (*jen*), wishing to be established himself, seeks also to establish others; wishing to be enlightened himself, seeks also to enlighten others
>
> (The Analects, 6, 28, 2)

Group orientation

Hofstede defined 'individualism' as pertaining to 'societies in which the ties between individuals are loose: everyone is expected to look after himself or herself and his or her immediate family'. He also defined 'collectivism' as pertaining to 'societies in which people from birth onwards are integrated into strong, cohesive in-groups, which throughout people's lifetime continue to protect them in exchange for unquestioning loyalty' (Hofstede, 1991: 51). According to his findings, Chinese societies are less individualistic, hence more collectivistic, than their Western counterparts. However, the Hofstede data were collected almost a quarter century before and there has been an abundance of cross-cultural research on individualism versus collectivism. Triandis and his colleagues have analyzed data collected from ten cultures which were labeled by Hofstede as either individualistic or collectivistic. The results indicated that Chinese societies still possess a high level of collectivism as compared to other cultures. For example, they found an extreme rejection to 'separation from in-groups' in Hong Kong and China; low scores for 'independence' in China; and very high scores for 'dependence' and 'family integrity' in Hong Kong and China. (Triandis *et al.*, 1993: 378–9).

There is probably no denial for the highly collectivistic nature of the Chinese culture. Some historical and cultural explanations discussed earlier serve also to explain this phenomenon. It is interesting to note here that Chinese collectivism has long been an important influence in Japanese culture. For example, most of the language used in the 'Seventeen Article Constitution' of Prince Shotoku were drawn from Confucian texts and much of the specific institutional arrangements were constructed based on Chinese models (de Bary, 1988: 31–2). In the last article, it was read: 'Matters should not be decided by one person alone. They should be discussed with many others. In small matters, of less consequence, many others need not be consulted. It is only in considering weighty matters, where there is a suspicion they might miscarry, that many others should be involved in debate and discussion so as to arrive at a reasonable judgment' (De Mente, 1991: 4–5).

Although it is true that Confucius did emphasize interdependence and group orientation, it is important here to explore the extent of the scope of the so-called 'group' in the Chinese sense. Confucius described the ideal society in terms of two stages namely, the first stage of 'small tranquillity' (*hsiao k'ang*), and the highest stage of 'great harmony' (*ta t'ung*). In the first stage, the family is the basis of social and political organization (Cheng, 1990: 195). True love (*jen*) as taught by Confucius is not yet achieved at this stage. When each one regards as his parents only his parents, and as his children only his children, universal and undifferentiated love would be impossible. The stage of great harmony represents the highest stage of social evolution when love permeates human society. Thus everyone loves all others, just as naturally as he loves his own parents or his children or himself. Everybody, regardless of age, sex, or different conditions of life, is properly taken care of by the society under a perfect system (p. 201).

It seems that the Chinese normally possess a narrower view of Confucius' great harmony. There is a distinction between the in-group (*zijiren*) and the out-group (*wairen*) for the Chinese (Gabrenya and Hwang, 1996: 311). The former is normally dominated by kinship, which represents the 'first, last, and only' source of security in traditional China (p. 310). However, the in-group often includes friends, colleagues, and co-workers whom Hwang (1987) described as members of the 'expressive ties'. The out-group clearly includes strangers, and of course, foreigners. Socialization from the out-group into the in-group is a matter of time and of course, *yuarn*. However, it is not to say that the Chinese way of clearly distinguishing between *zijiren* and *wairen* will lead the former to treat the latter in inhuman or unjust ways. Based on the belief in harmony and propriety, people treat one another by *li*. The following quote from *The Analects* is clear about the point.

> Sima Niu said sadly, 'All men have brothers, I alone have none!' Zixia said, 'I have heard that life and death are determined by fate, that wealth and honors depend upon the will of Heaven. A superior man attends to business carefully and does not trip; he is respectful to others and observant of propriety. All within the world will be his brothers. How can a superior man feel distressed about his lack of them?'
>
> (The Analects, 12, 5)

Continuity

Yau (1994: 79) quoted the popular Chinese proverb 'If you have been my teacher for a day, I will treat you like my father forever' to demonstrate the Chinese belief that inter-relations with objects and people are continuous. Based on their emphasis on respect for authority and filial piety, as well as *yuarn*, it appears natural that such a sense of continuity should prevail. The value can be appropriately analyzed in terms of two aspects namely, loyalty to the superior and the attitude towards learning. In the organization, an employee expends effort at work not only because of the instrumental attractiveness of the job, but also of his or her moral commitment to fulfill a duty and to contribute to the collectivity

(Hui and Tan, 1996). This is not only a reflection of the Confucian emphasis on loyalty (*chung*) between the sovereign and the servant, but also a manifestation of the emphasis on reciprocity (*pao*), the repayment of a favor by the recipient (Yau, 1994; Hui and Tan, 1996). Thus, relationships between superiors and subordinates, teachers and students, parents and sons are naturally continuous. In the past, and also commonly in the present, continuity extends beyond a lifetime as exemplified in the Chinese emphasis on ancestral worship and burial and mourning rituals. Given this emphasis on continued relationships with things and people, the Chinese see particular importance in perpetual learning, which has been the central doctrine of Confucius. It is a commonly accepted principle in life the popular Chinese saying 'There is no end to learning'. The following quotes from Confucius are clear.

> Is it not pleasant to learn with a constant perseverance and application? Is it not delightful to have friends coming from distant quarters? Is he not a man of complete virtue, who feels no discomposure though men may not take note of him?
>
> (The Analects, 1, 1)

> The philosopher Tsang said, 'I daily examine myself on three points: whether, in transacting business for others, I may have been not faithful; whether, in intercourse with friends, I may have been not sincere; whether I may have not mastered and practiced the instructions of my teacher.'
>
> (The Analects 1, 4)

Past time orientation

The Chinese have been well-known for their being conservative and historically-minded as compared to most Westerners. Kluckhohn and Strodtbeck (1961: 14–15) pointed out that historical China was a society which gave preference to past time orientation while the Americans place an emphasis upon the future more strongly than other people. This is true as manifested by the Chinese emphasis on respect for authority and filial piety as discussed in the previous section.

This past time orientation does have its positive aspect. On administering a Chinese version of the Morris and Jones (1955) 'Ways to Live' survey to Chinese university students in Taiwan, Yang (1972; cited in Yang, 1986: 119) found that the respondents ranked the highest preference rating for way number one namely, 'Preserve the best that man has attained'. In reality, it is known that the Chinese are vigilant in learning good things from history and are keen in preserving them. Even Confucius himself was an enthusiastic learner who took good examples from the past. In order to make his teaching more authoritative and effective, Confucius had sometimes to borrow the authority of the ancient ideal rulers (Cheng, 1990: 192). The following quote from *The Great Learning* typically exemplifies the importance of learning from the past.

> In the Books of Poetry, it is said, 'Ah! the former kings are not forgotten.' Future princes deem worthy what they deemed worthy, and love what they loved. The common people delight in what delighted them, and are benefited by their beneficial arrangements. It is on this account that the former kings, after they have quitted the world, are not forgotten.
>
> (The Great Learning)

The Doctrine of the Mean and harmony with others

'The Doctrine of the Mean' (*Chung Yung*) is one of the essential teachings of Confucius which has been embraced by the Chinese until the present. All his teachings were consistent with this doctrine. In his teachings on love (*jen*) or the rules of propriety (*li*) or filial piety (*hsiao*), he emphasized both social and individual, motive and consequence, mind and action, as well as acquired experiences and innate tendencies (Cheng, 1990: 288). Confucius mentioned about 'the state of equilibrium' where there are no stirrings of pleasure, anger, sorrow, or joy. Practicing the doctrine is an example of cultivating moral virtue for the self. Not following the mean leads to distortion in social harmony as well as moral deterioration.

> Confucius said, 'The Superior Man embodies the course of the Mean; the mean man acts contrary to the course of the Mean.'
>
> (The Doctrine of the Mean, 2, 1)

> The superior man accords with the course of the Mean. Though he may be all unknown, disregarded by the world, he feels no regret. It is only the sage who is able for this.
>
> (The Doctrine of the Mean, 2, 1)

In other words, the value is manifested in a balanced life. A virtuous man will never allow himself to be led astray by extreme desires or passions. He would rather be led by common sense than by any unprofitable adventures (Cheng, 1990: 289). Therefore, the Chinese are taught not to let primitive passions and impulses be completely repressed or unrestrictedly satisfied (Yau, 1994: 80–1) for this will disrupt harmony with others. In *The Analects*, the following quote is clear.

> Zigong asked, 'Who is better, Shi or Shang?' The Master said, 'Shi goes too far; Shang goes not far enough.' Zigong said, 'Than Shi is better, I suppose.' The Master said, 'Too far is no better than not far enough.'
>
> (The Analects, 11, 16)

This ethical way of being was found to be reflected in Yang's (1972) administration of the Morris and Jones (1955) 'Ways to Live' survey in which the respondents ranked a high preference rating for way number ten namely, 'Control the self stoically.' (Yang, 1986: 119).

Modern Chinese cultural values

After a rather detailed explanation of some important Chinese cultural values, the question of whether such apparently traditional values still prevail nowadays has to be addressed. Given the Chinese have been constantly influenced by societal modernization, it is obvious that a possibility of change in basic values exists. The following discussion attempts to answer the question by persuading that the fundamental values of the Chinese are still relevant today. This is largely a result of constant reinforcement of traditional values in the education system and even in the national directives of Chinese societies. Though there may be changes, they should actually be thought of in terms of the degree of change. It must be emphasized again here that underlying values do not change drastically as raised in the theories of Rokeach (1973), Hofstede and Bond (1988), and Yau (1994), which the present study has strictly adhered to.

The discussion starts firstly with a brief overview of the relevance of Confucian moral values to Chinese societies nowadays. Perhaps the most obvious and appealing example is the impact of Confucianism on Singapore, which is dominated by ethnic Chinese for around 77 per cent of the total population. Lu (1983: 88–9) strongly believed that although most Singaporean Chinese are English-educated, they still retain contacts with their traditional values through familial and social associations. Many may doubt that Confucian values are today incompatible with modern science, technology and economic growth. However, the question depends very much on how people look at the matter (p. 89).

The Singaporean Government has been concerned with preserving traditional values by constantly reinforcing them through various official blessings. For example, in reinforcing family cohesiveness and filial piety, special priority in housing allocation are given to those who live with their parents (p. 86). In terms of political leadership, Mr Lee Kuan Yew, former Prime Minister of Singapore, spelt out basic principles based on Confucian values for leaders to follow (p. 102). Lu argued that such promotions do not aim at introducing 'new values' to the people because Confucian values have always been influential (p. 91). In other words, the underlying value assumptions of the modern ethnic Chinese Singaporeans are still Confucian in nature. Clearly enough, there has been an overall tendency for Singapore to preserve what is good for the moral development of its people. Lu further argued that it is enough to follow the Confucian perspective and to be inspired by the Confucian moral examples. It would be actually against the spirit of Confucianism to follow the minute details of Confucian moral codes (p. 108).

It is believed that a similar situation can be found in other Chinese societies like Hong Kong and Taiwan. Although unlike Singapore which uses direct governmental interventions, reinforcement of Confucian values can be seen mostly in the form of formally integrating the Confucian classics in most Chinese primary and secondary school texts. The child is often encouraged to memorize the classics and to manifest his learning through building relationships based on Confucian principles. Redding (1990: 48) argued that Confucian education is nevertheless still a major force in Hong Kong, a dominant one in Taiwan, and an officially sponsored one in Singapore. Even in mainland China today, classical Confucian teachings are often contained in textbooks used by primary schools and even international schools.

It is probably the latent characteristic of cultural values which has made the modern Chinese to be unaware of its existence. That is also a possible reason why Chinese societies are constantly reinforcing such values in different ways. There is no doubt that Confucian traditionalism remains, but in new contexts (Redding, 1990: 52). Confucianism is not simply a creed which has been selected from some competing phil-osophies; it is a way of life encompassing the ultimate standards for Chinese social and political order. Confucianism for China represents the most powerful and universally accepted indigenous tradition, one that is irreplaceable by even Taoism and Buddhism (Smith, 1973: 232).

The argument that traditional Chinese cultural values are still relevant and active in the hearts of the modern Chinese can also be supported by citing the findings of several authoritative studies. Bond (1996) pointed out three important studies of values at the cultural level relevant to the present discussion. They are the Hofstede (1980) project, the Chinese value survey (The Chinese Culture Connection, 1987), and the Schwartz value survey (Schwartz and Bilsky, 1987; 1990).

The Hofstede project revealed that Chinese societies like Hong Kong, Taiwan, and Singapore were united in their high power distance, low individualism, low uncertainty avoidance, and medium masculinity ratings. Similarly, the Chinese value survey showed that Singapore, Taiwan, and Hong Kong were high on Confucian work dynamism. The Schwartz survey found the mainland Chinese especially high on the importance of attribution to hierarchy and master values. Of course, differences among the four major Chinese societies were found. However, such findings are quite sufficient to persuade that the modern Chinese do possess Confucian-type cultural values. Bond (1996) even further integrated the findings of the three surveys and came up with four factors namely: (1) Individualism–Hierarchy (the opposition of universalistic, open values with traditional, authoritarian emphases); (2) Orderly Autonomy (a strong emphasis on stability as well as individual freedom); (3) Discipline-Assertion (the focus of achievement and satisfaction as opposed by an emphasis on restraint and a long-term focus); and (4) Achievement factor (emphasis on achievement-oriented concerns). From the results, there appears to be an emphasis representing the enduring features of Confucianism. At the same time, the results also hinted on the influence by new value orientations. Although it is quite comfortable to conclude here that traditional Chinese cultural values are still relevant and active, it would be wise to remain conservative by pointing out and accepting that there have been certain changes due to societal modernization. However, the changes here refer to a matter of degree. In other words, the fundamental essences still remain.

Yang, after reviewing numerous studies on Chinese personality conducted since 1948, concluded that there have been both increasing and decreasing trends in some important evaluative–attitudinal characteristics of the Chinese personality. For example, preference for achievement, individualistic relationship, self-indulgence, aesthetic values, belief for internal control, and democratic attitudes are among the increasing trend. Preference for inner development, collective relationship, social restraint and self-control, theoretical, social, and religious values, belief for external-control, and authoritarian attitudes have been decreasing (Yang, 1986: 161). Yang (1996: 487–8) then expanded the list to include some 30 evaluative–attitudinal characteristics with decreasing emphasis and 27 with increasing emphasis. In general, he argued that the decreasing characteristics may be summarized under the concept of the social-oriented personality and those increasing under the concept of the individual-oriented personality. These changes appear inevitable. However, Confucianism, like capitalism, is a matter of what one does. Its power is widespread and extremely difficult to delineate (Redding, 1990: 47). Nevertheless, it should be remembered that Confucian traditionalism have been shaken off, counteracted, or subtly amended in the course of history. One thing is clear, the tradition still remains but probably in new contexts (p. 52).

4
The Theory of Culture-specific TQM

In this chapter, drawing from the discussions on TQM and Chinese cultural values in Chapters 2 and 3, some likely relationships between them are postulated. Then, relevant studies involving the constructs of TQM and Chinese culture are critically reviewed. Gathering all these on the premise of the emic–etic analysis as presented in Chapter 1, a framework for the culture-specific TQM by extending Anderson *et al.*'s (1994) TQM theorization is developed for further operationalization.

Likely relationships between Chinese cultural values and TQM

Based on a derived etic approach, if one studies carefully the spirit of TQM and the core principles of the Chinese cultural values, it is possible to delineate some relationships between them. The likely links are briefly explained here.

(1) *Harmony with nature*: In the context of modern business activities, 'nature' here can be viewed as the worldwide arena of commercial competition. Thus, this value is of particular importance for enhancing adaptation to the worldwide market need for quality. In order to adapt to the 'nature', the creation of appropriate visions and organizational cultures essential to maintain the adaptation becomes a need for subsistence and survival.

(2) *Yuarn*: As the Chinese believe in *yuarn*, it is likely that they tend to emphasize harmonious relationships both within and outside the organization. This helps to enhance inter-departmental communication and cooperation. Also, customer satisfaction and supplier relationships are highly valued. The concept of 'face' is also believed to be highly constructive towards such orientations.

(3) *Abasement*: The value of abasement leads people to be humble and sincere. Thus, it is an essential agent in encouraging people at all levels to learn new philosophies and to acquire new work skills. Also, quality leadership can be instituted with more ease when employees are sincere and willing to learn. In this respect, organizational leaders cannot simply provide tacit spiritual guidance. Rather, they are 'down to earth' and have to fully involve and participate in organizational endeavors in order to demonstrate real life examples of the virtuous father-like figure.

(4) *Situation orientation*: The pragmatic orientation of the Chinese builds a sound foundation for them to accept scientific ways to manage quality. Statistical process control, problem solving tools, standardization, and ISO 9000 implementation are thus readily accepted. Furthermore, the Western quantum leap or pure innovation approach is not congruent with Chinese cultural values (Martinsons and Hempel 1998). Rather, the emphasis is on adapting and refining foreign technologies so as to build up a unique system. Thus, the institutional arrangements of good Western management practices are highly acknowledged in structuring the organizational system while it is contextualized by underlying Chinese cultural values.

(5) *Respect for authority*: As quality has to be largely an initiative from top management, the respect for hierarchical authorities helps to enhance lower level managers and employees to adhere to directives given from above. Thus, the organizational climate in a Chinese TQM company is represented by a fusion between the paternalistic and hierarchical relationships as in Confucian principles and the participative management style as advocated in TQM. The essence is to use the former to act as a boundary within which the latter works so as to maintain a harmonious family-like organization.

(6) *Interdependence*: As TQM can be successful only if organization-wide commitment is present, the value of interdependence serves to enhance unity of organizational objectives. Employees can be educated that quality activities help not only themselves, but also others, thus enhancing involvement.

(7) *Group orientation*: This value is clearly constructive towards the implementation of quality control circles and other group activities. Collective rather than individual talents are more encouraged. Neither the Western individualistic 'one champion' approach nor the Japanese-style voluntarism are directly applicable.

(8) *Continuity*: The long-term orientation of the Chinese is perfectly in line with TQM's need for continuous efforts in quality improvement (*kaizen*), continuous learning, and continuous evaluation.

(9) *Past time orientation*: To preserve what is good in the past is the foundation for continuous improvement. In the context of the PDCA cycle, employees are likely to emphasize on the 'check' part (reflections), leading to further improving already acceptable records of quality achievement.

(10) *The Doctrine of the Mean and harmony with others*: When people avoid going into extremes by following the mean, they tend to become self-disciplined. Work disciplines and work standardization are thus readily accepted. When harmony in the workplace is valued, employees express mutual respect. This not only enhances employee satisfaction, but it can also be extended outside the organization to create an orientation towards customer satisfaction and supplier cooperation.

Table 4.1 attempts to map out the likely relationships mentioned. Those Chinese cultural values likely to be in line with or constructive to TQM implementation and practices are depicted. However, it should be noted that although dividing lines have been used, it is not necessary that a particular cultural value is adjacent to certain TQM philosophies or practices. In other words, the relationships among the elements in each row are not linked exclusively. Furthermore, there may be combinations of values which are positive towards certain TQM interventions. For the time being, such likely linkages between Chinese cultural values and TQM remain mere speculations. Evidences need to be collected from the literature and generated from the present empirical study.

Table 4.1   Likely links between Chinese cultural values and TQM

Chinese cultural values	TQM philosophy and practices
Harmony with nature	Adaptation to the worldwide demand for quality
	Quality vision and quality culture
Yuarn	Pursuit for internal and external customer satisfaction
	Inter-departmental communication
	Supplier quality and loyalty
Abasement	Quality leadership
	Obsession to learning
Situation orientation	Scientific approach to quality management
	Statistical process control and problem solving tools
	Standardization and ISO 9000
Respect for authority	Top management leadership in quality
Interdependence	Unity of purpose
	Involvement in quality programs
Group orientation	Teamwork
	Quality control circles
	Group dynamics

Continuity	Long-term commitment to quality
	Continuous improvement (*kaizen*)
	Continuous learning
	Continuous evaluation
Past time orientation	Learning from experience
	Continuous improvement (*kaizen*)
	Plan-do-check-act (PDCA) cycle
Doctrine of the Mean	Standardization
	Work discipline
Harmony with others	Internal and external customer satisfaction
	Job satisfaction and enrichment

Previous studies on TQM in a Chinese context

Total quality management and Chinese cultural values as the two main subjects of the present study have been examined to some length. It is now appropriate to associate them together. However, before attempting to develop a theory to explain the inter-relationships between Chinese cultural values and TQM, a critical review of several studies which have attempted to analyze TQM in a Chinese cultural context is conducted.

As pointed out in Chapter 1, studies on the influence of national culture on TQM are scarce. Studies which have specifically associated Chinese cultural values and TQM are even more difficult to find. On the other hand, studies which have employed samples of Chinese companies in regions such as Hong Kong and Taiwan are not difficult to locate. For example, Chen (1997) employed a sample of 105 Taiwanese companies to examine the leadership and human resource management aspects of TQM in Taiwan. Although the author did not analyze specifically how Taiwanese culture as an indigenous one affects such managerial processes in TQM, he has appropriately signaled the need to examine human factors underlying TQM in Chinese regions as the economy of the Asia Pacific rim has become increasingly important.

In another study by the same author (Chen and Lu, 1998), the importance to look into traditional Chinese cultural values, namely Confucian values in TQM, was highlighted. The authors argued that there is no universal model of quality transformation and culture does matter in the implementation of TQM. Conducting an in-depth analysis of one Taiwanese company, the authors demonstrated how TQM could be effectively implemented by following 'The Great Learning', an important ancient Confucian philosophy. Though the study has illustrated the fact that Chinese philosophy may play an important role in guiding the Chinese firm along the path of quality transformation, the coverage of the various important Chinese values is clearly insufficient.

Recognizing this obvious research gap, Jenner *et al.* (1998) conducted in-depth interviews with ten joint ventures between American firms and Chinese state enterprises. The objective was to assess whether the cultural attributes of Chinese state enterprises constitute serious obstacles to the introduction of TQM. The findings are intriguing although some areas warrant a critical review.

Firstly, the researchers interviewed only the American managers of the joint ventures and concluded that nine out of the ten joint ventures were felt under-performing by the American managers. In particular, the American managers attributed the reason to that the culture of the Chinese partners could not be reformed (Jenner *et al.*, 1998: 194). This conclusion is questionable. Based on the emic–etic theory as discussed in Chapter 1, these joint ventures are hybrids. Concluding that the culture of the Chinese partners does not fuse properly with TQM from the viewpoint of the American managers is probably an imposed-etic approach. A comprehensive approach should start with an imposed-etic process whereby the researchers look into the joint ventures from an American viewpoint. After this, they should draw out the emics or specifics of the American as well as Chinese cultures. Lastly, they should then draw out the commonalities or etics of the two systems. Of course, differences between the two distinct systems can also be identified during this stage thus determining whether diversity is high or low. However, the researchers have only investigated from an imposed-etic viewpoint, thus 'Americanizing' TQM and ignoring the transcendent nature of TQM as a culture itself.

Another area which warrants clarification is their argument that TQM can be used as an agent for cultural transformation in the Chinese state-owned enterprises. This argument appears sound and true indeed. However, there are doubts concerning the process of cultural trans-formation as stated by the researchers. They pointed out that one out of the ten joint ventures interviewed had successfully implemented TQM and used it as a change agent in transforming the enterprise's culture. What they argued as its reason of success is rather than attempting to change the culture of the Chinese enterprise before implementing TQM, this enterprise implemented TQM first. Given the imposed-etic view-point of the researchers, the above method merely meant a replacement of the Chinese cultural values by the Americanized TQM culture in the enterprise. Based on Uemura (1998) and Abo's (1994) theories, a hybrid arises as a fusion of two systems but not a complete absorption of one by the other. Although the internalization theory states that the more advantageous aspects of one system will be taken over by the other, it is the central idea of the present study to argue that a successful hybrid should be able to mutually absorb the advantageous aspects of each other. If one system completely absorbs the other or if one system has to completely transform in order to adapt to the other, there is nothing called a hybrid then. In other words, American-style TQM, Japanese-style TQM, and Chinese-style TQM will all be the same.

The researchers then went on to point out five cultural aspects of the Chinese state enterprise which are inconsistent with five major TQM principles (Jenner *et al.*, 1998: 196–201). Firstly, Confucianism and Maoism tend to value stability over change. The former also encourages formal patterns of communication within a hierarchical structure. This is inconsistent with TQM's avocation of management as providers of support towards continuous improvement. Secondly, influenced by Maoism, Chinese state enterprises focus on serving the needs of the state rather than those of internal and external customers as in TQM. Thirdly, Confucianism and Maoism discourage free expression of ideas while TQM requires commitment of all workers in the organization. Fourthly, influenced by Maoism, Chinese state enterprises tend to isolate workers and to discourage worker participation. Any deviations from the official doctrines are not allowed, distrust is created. On the other hand, TQM requires all organizational units to continually improve and to drive out fear. Finally, influenced by Confucianism, Chinese enterprises tend to discourage alliances with any organizations which do not have close familial ties with key employees. However, TQM requires all organizations associated with the enterprise to equally involve in continuous improvement.

To support the above incompatibilities, the researchers cited many examples of Maoist communist practices in the state enterprises. This is not necessarily appropriate because many of these practices have become irrelevant after the reform of the state enterprises which began in the early 1980s. As Laaksonen (1988) and Child (1994) have already pointed out, the economic reform since Deng Xiaopeng's open door policy has brought the management of Chinese enterprises into another era. Nevertheless, due to the imposed etic approach that the researchers have employed, many of the underlying Chinese cultural values have became obstacles instead of opportunities for the successful implementation of TQM. Of course, one should not ignore the possibility that many Chinese state enterprises may still adhere to certain communist practices. In fact many of them still appear as giant 'monsters' with an urgent need of reform. However, as revealed later on in the case studies conducted, managers of Chinese enterprises are admitting that such past practices are no more appropriate at present. Furthermore, they are gradually revisiting the important Confucian traits which are more in line with fundamental TQM principles. It is obviously healthier to employ a derived etic approach in which commonalities between Chinese culture and TQM are identified so as to better understand the characteristics of the Chinese-style TQM. Generally speaking, Jenner and colleagues have raised some possible difficulties in implementing TQM in a Chinese setting. Their findings are undoubtedly practical and valuable. However, as a study of cultural influences on TQM, it has focused more on cultural manifestations rather than underlying cultural values.

Another study which has systematically designed a Chinese culture-specific research instrument to test the association of Confucian values and TQM was conducted by Lo (1998, 1999). Claimed to be the first attempt to investigate the appropriateness of using Confucian principles in quality management in Chinese-based organizations, Lo found out that Chinese managers do find Confucian principles relevant in managing quality, and they do practice them in reality. Following the Fishbein behavioral intention model (Fishbein and Ajzen, 1975), he designed an instrument composed of 19 Confucian principles and administered it to 90 Chinese managers in Hong Kong. In particular, he identified two areas in which Chinese staff and managers feel positive towards the successful implementation of TQM. The first is the importance of a strong leadership through the Confucian trait of *de*, which means virtue, goodness, kindness, morality, favor, or ethics. In order to have faithful followers, they believe that it is important for quality managers to act in accordance with the commonly accepted ethical values and principles governing the conduct of the group (Lo, 1999: 552). Another important area is the ability to work in harmony through the existence of a well-balanced hierarchy in the company. This hierarchical relationship helps to identify the roles and responsibilities of every member which in turn lead to mutual and complementary obligations and cooperation.

Lo's study was probably still in its preliminary stage and thus warranted further analyses and replications to ensure reliability. It is also a pity that only two areas of importance were identified namely, leadership and harmony. Comparing the findings of Jenner *et al.* and Lo, it is interesting to see that the former employed an imposed etic view on the association of Chinese cultural values and TQM, and the latter, an emic view. The findings are nearly opposite. For instance, Lo found that Chinese staff and managers actually favored a formal hierarchical organization and they felt that this is positive towards the implementation of TQM. On the other hand, Jenner *et al.* suggested that the hierarchical structure inhibits communication among the organizational members. Lo indicated that a paternalistic leadership based on Confucian traits is essential for a successful TQM endeavor while Jenner *et al.* argued that this obstructs innovation and participation by organizational members. These two examples have appropriately signaled the need for more emic or derived etic studies on the association of Chinese cultural values and TQM.

To date, perhaps Roney's (1997) study is more objective and derived etic in nature. In analyzing the relationship between Polish culture and TQM, consistencies as well as inconsistencies between the two were identified. In line with the present research, she proposed management not to attempt to change the host culture in order to pave way for the successful implementation of alien management approaches such as TQM. Rather, a systematic evaluation of the inconsistencies will facilitate a flexible and successful planning and implementation. As she concluded in her study, changes will occur in Polish firms, and they may resemble the values of TQM, but it will likely be in Poland's own image, signifying the emergence of a distinct hybrid, or Polish-style TQM.

Another discussion of a similar vein can be found in Martinsons (1996) and Martinsons and Hempel (1998). In comparing the fundamental Confucian values and the principles behind business process reengineering (BPR), the authors raised a series of propositions stating that Chinese organizations will find more difficulties than their American counterparts in implementing BPR. In particular, due to the underlying Chinese cultural values, Chinese organizations tend to find it more difficult to implement formal process planning, formal process models, and process-based performance appraisals. Also, difficulties are expected at the need to make quantum leaps from the *status quo* and to apply radical and disruptive forms of process change. On the other hand, it was expected that Chinese organizations will find it easier than their American counterparts to implement work teams. Nevertheless, the authors warned that the implementation of 'genuine' BPR would require tremendous and unprecedented changes in the fundamental values of the Chinese (Martinsons and Hempel, 1998: 405). As such, BPR has to be reinterpreted as it diffuses into the Chinese business context and there should be a Chinese-style BPR which will encompass less formal planning and documentation, more gradual implementations, and more authoritarian management (p. 407). This Chinese-style BPR will vary significantly from the 'genuine' American BPR. This objective discussion of the need to reinterpret BPR principles is much in line with the mutual fusion effect between Chinese cultural values and TQM as argued in the present study.

Developing the theory of culture-specific TQM

In Chapter 1, the theorization of TQM, especially in terms of a human and cultural foundation, has been underscored. A review of a handful of attempts to theorize TQM revealed that there can be two main approaches namely, 'to borrow from without' and 'to borrow from within' (Chiles and Choi, 2000: 187). Chiles and Choi's (2000) attempt to theorize TQM by drawing convergence between TQM and Austrian market process economics is an example of developing theories by importing ideas from 'without'. Their motive of using a borrowing from 'without' approach can be understood because much has been said about the prescriptive and atheoretical nature of TQM itself. Thus, building TQM theory by borrowing from something which is itself unstable appears risky. However, it is argued here that the lack of convergence in TQM principles is fundamentally a question of how people think TQM should be. Or more precisely, how people want TQM to be. That is to say, the excessive belief in the universality of TQM and a lack of concern as to the contingent nature of management theories. This perspective on TQM is in fact unfair and it probably stems from our good old ethnocentric tradition of management research. Therefore, if the 'within' of TQM is not properly treated with an appropriate research attitude requiring an attention to human and cultural factors, any further experiments to borrow from 'without' will only lead to more inconsistencies and debates.

So, going back to the 'within' again, the theorization of TQM started with the identification and measurement of its underlying factors. Saraph *et al.*'s (1989) study represents an early and authoritative attempt of this type. After reviewing the quality management literature according to Deming (1986), Juran (1951), Ishikawa (1964), Crosby (1979), Garvin (1983, 1984), Leonard and Sasser (1982), Mondon (1982), and Adam *et al.* (1981), the researchers identified eight critical factors of quality management. After a series of rigorous reliability and validity testing, an instrument to measure these factors evolved. The eight factors are namely: (1) role of divisional top management and quality policy; (2) role of the quality department; (3) training; (4) product/service design; (5) supplier quality management; (6) process management/operating procedures;

(7) quality data and reporting; and (8) employee relations. Saraph *et al.* called for more endeavors to replicate their scale or to design better instruments to measure underlying TQM elements. Since then, attempts such as Flynn *et al.* (1994), Black and Porter (1996) and Grandzol and Gershon (1998) could be seen contributing and extending the work of Saraph *et al.* Although briefly mentioned at the end of a related paper (Flynn *et al.*, 1995) that management needs to carefully assess an organization's culture in matching TQM elements [by citing Hall (1983) that some American plant workers felt the Japanese *kanban* silly], these attempts at devising measurement instruments of TQM clearly tended towards the universalistic assumption of TQM interventions and the ethnocentric research tradition. To our delight, three inter-related studies conducted mainly by John C. Anderson, Manus Rungtusanatham, and Roger C. Shroeder have demonstrated a process for the TQM research community to gradually recognize the drawbacks of the universalistic assumption and research ethnocentrism. This 'trilogy' includes theory development (Anderson *et al.*, 1994), empirical testing (Anderson *et al.*, 1995), and replication (Rungtusanatham *et al.*, 1998) of a TQM theory underlying the Deming management method which we conveniently denote here as the 'ARS theory'. The three episodes are now briefly reviewed.

ARS theory: theory development

In response to the Academy of Management's noticing that there has been a lack of theory development for TQM, Anderson *et al.* (1994) published an article entitled 'A theory of quality management underlying the Deming management method' in the *Academy of Management Review's* special issue on total quality. Recognizing the importance of Deming in the TQM movement and the wide acceptance of his '14 points', the researchers doubted whether labeling the 14 points as 'the Deming theory of management' is appropriate. They found that the 14 points merely provided the 'whats' or building blocks of a theory. It was necessary to establish the 'how?' and 'why?' of the theory (p. 477). To tackle this, they proposed a three-phase theory generation method. Firstly, a preliminary set of concepts was generated through employing the Delphi method. This involved the derivation of 37 concepts from the 14 points by a panel of seven experts from academe and industry. Through further abstractions, the 37 concepts were grouped under seven major concepts namely: (1) visionary leadership; (2) internal and external cooperation; (3) learning; (4) process management; (5) continuous improvement; (6) employee fulfillment; and (7) customer satisfaction

(p. 480). Detailed definitions of these concepts were then derived from the literature.

The second phase of theory development involved identifying the conceptual relationships among the seven main concepts so as to answer the 'how?' of the theory. With the help of relations diagrams, Anderson *et al.* proposed a process-type theory articulating causal directions and feedback mechanisms (p. 481). In the form of propositions, the ARS theory was stipulated as follows:

Proposition 1: Visionary leadership enables the simultaneous creation of a cooperative and learning organization.
Proposition 2: An organization that simultaneously fosters cooperation and learning facilitates the implementation of process management practices.
Proposition 3: Process management practices simultaneously result in continuous improvement of quality and employee fulfillment.
Proposition 4: An organization's simultaneous efforts continuously to improve its quality and to fulfill its employees lead to higher customer satisfaction.

The third phase of theory development involved juxtaposing the concepts and conceptual relationships against existing literature. This is a borrowing from 'without' kind of theory generation process and was fused together with the previous two phases which represented a borrowing from 'within' kind of method. To this end, Anderson *et al.* juxtaposed the proposed ARS theory against Taylor's (1911) principles of scientific management and Lawrence and Dyer's (1983) theory of readaptative organizations. Through this three-phase process, the ARS theory represents a well-grounded theory appropriately addressing the 'what?', 'how?', and 'why?' of the theory of quality management.

ARS theory: empirical testing

Continuing the journey of theory development, Anderson *et al.* (1995) published in *Decision Sciences* their empirical test of the ARS theory.

In order to operationalize the seven theoretical constructs of the ARS theory, a multi-item perceptual scale based on the previous work of Flynn *et al.* (1994) was designed. The instrument was administered to 41 manufacturing plants in the United States. The seven theoretical constructs all yielded Cronbach's αs of at least 0.60. Path analysis was used to test the relationships in the process-type ARS theory. The four propositions depicted earlier were thus operationalized into the following 'causal' relations which could be assessed through hypothesis testing:

Proposition 1: Path 1a (visionary leadership → internal and external cooperation)
Path 1b (visionary leadership → learning)
Proposition 2: Path 2a (internal and external cooperation → process management)
Path 2b (learning → process management)
Proposition 3: Path 3a (process management → continuous improvement)
Path 3b (process management → employee fulfillment)
Proposition 4: Path 4a (continuous improvement → customer satisfaction)
Path 4b (employee fulfillment → customer satisfaction)

The findings revealed that all the paths were statistically significant except paths 2b and 4a. Such results were attributed to reasons of statistical problems and data inadequacy. Generally speaking, the researchers concluded that most relationships in the ARS theory were supported but room for improvement and extension existed. Unfortunately, they did not provide the overall explained variance of the model which could have been obtained as a goodness-of-fit index if structural equation modeling were used instead. Replications assessing the cross-cultural validity of the theory was also called for. In fact, the sample included both American-owned as well as Japanese-owned plants. But the researchers did not attempt to test the validity of the theory in these two sub-samples.

ARS theory: replication

The third episode in the trilogy was a replication study of the ARS theory (Rungtusanatham *et al.*, 1998) published in the *Journal of Operations Management*. With a clear objective to examine the universal applicability of quality management, the researchers challenged the 'one size fits all' assumption by replicating the ARS theory testing in an Italian context, 43 manufacturing plants in Italy participated in the study. All conditions and methodologies were maintained as similar as possible to those in the Anderson *et al.* (1995) study using American plants. Out of the eight paths as described in the last section, only paths 1a, 1b, 2a, 3a and 4a were statistically significant (paths 1b and 4a were partially significant with *p* values minimally beyond the level of 0.05). Therefore, in terms of the four theoretical propositions, only proposition 1 received full empirical support while the remaining three propositions received mixed support (Rungtusanatham *et al.*, 1998: 86).

In explaining such a result, the researchers pinpointed that the ARS theory was the product of a parochial study, a research conducted in one culture by researchers of that culture (Rungtusanatham *et al.*, 1998: 87). Borrowing support from Adler (1983), they argued that ethnocentric research designs are often applicable only to one culture, that is the culture in which the research was conducted. Due to differences between the American and Italian cultures, it was not confirmed that the ARS theory is universally applicable. Following the advice of Adler, the researchers also reckoned that even if similar findings were found in a two-culture study, the claim of universality is still unwarranted. Nevertheless, they concluded with the empirical support of proposition 1 that some relationships in the ARS theory could be applied to describe, explain, and predict quality management beyond the American culture. For example, in both cultures, organizational leaders are critical in developing and communicating a vision which facilitates cooperation and learning. Thus it will be easier to implement process-oriented management practices. This is true indeed. However, the researchers failed to provide a cultural explanation as to why it is easier to implement process-oriented management practices with such a cooperative vision given from top leaders. Which cultural value is likely to contribute towards this facility? The problem here appears to be a lack of juxtaposing empirical findings against social and cultural theories. For instance, proposition 1 may hold in the context of Chinese culture due to its salient value of 'respect for authority'. Similarly, there must also be an American or an Italian cultural explanation of this. Going back to the central argument of the present research, each culture must fuse with TQM, giving rise to individually unique culture-specific TQM systems.

Four-proposition framework of the culture-specific TQM

As mentioned before, the universalistic assumption of TQM stems from its atheoretical and prescriptive nature as well as a parochial or ethnocentric research paradigm. In fact, even advocates of TQM universalism find difficulties in avoiding the element of culture. For example, Choi and Liker (1995) studied the implementation of Japanese continuous improvement (CI) approaches to American manufacturing. They started with the assumption that CI in manufacturing is not bounded by national culture (p. 590). Using a mixture of quantitative and qualitative methods, the researchers analyzed data gathered from manufacturing plants in the United States. They concluded that in implementing Japanese CI, it is the 'culture of work' which matters more than national culture. On the other hand, the researchers also admitted that since they did not obtain comparative data from Japanese plants, 'it is possible that a much larger proportion of Japanese plants would include a large proportion of process-oriented managers, and this is due to a national culture influence' (p. 609). This is clearly contradictory to their beginning assumption of universalism. Recht and Wilderom (1998) conducted a similar analysis on the transferability of Japanese suggestion systems to organizations outside Japan. Comparing Japanese *kaizen* with Hofstede's (1991) organizational culture dimensions, the researchers concluded that a successful transfer of *kaizen*-oriented suggestion system is less dependent on national culture than on organizational culture.

Two points may be raised here. Firstly, both Choi and Liker (1995) and Recht and Wilderom (1998) started with the assumption that continuous improvement and suggestion systems are 'Japanese'. This is witnessed with their labels of 'Japanese CI' and 'Japanese suggestion systems' in their article titles. This is difficult to assert as we have already argued in Chapters 1 and 2 that TQM is not a peculiar product of the Japanese and that TQM is a culture itself of a transcendent nature, not inclining towards any particular culture. Even if we follow the logic posed by Choi and Liker that TQM originated from the United States by Deming and was exported to Japan, we cannot assume that now 'Japanese TQM' is being reimported to the United States and is being run there. The reason is that when TQM was exported to Japan, the Japanese had already incorporated their own cultural traits into it, forming a hybrid-type TQM. Similarly, when it is to be reimported to the States, another adjustment to the new local context is required. Garvin (1986) warned that any attempts by American firms to mimic Japanese quality practices without adjustments are unlikely to succeed. Thus it is of limited use to label any TQM technique as 'Japanese' when it is in fact being implemented in the States or other countries. It is probably more constructive to see how the Japanese and the Americans run suggestions systems or CI similarly or differently. Unfortunately, the two articles did not provide cross-cultural data for comparison.

The second point is on their argument that national culture is less important than organizational culture on TQM implementation. First of all, it is very clear that the influence of organizational culture on TQM is of extreme importance. This can be witnessed by the discussions in Chapter 1 on quality cultures and the role of management to express inward cultures into concrete TQM interventions. However, according to our understanding of the sociological approach to organizations suggested by Parsons (1956), the sub-value system is always influenced by the super-ordinate system. Therefore, we argue for the unique existence of American-style TQM, Japanese-style TQM, and Chinese-style TQM. This argument has been well-articulated in Chapter 1 already. It is probably more conservative to say that both national and organizational cultures are important towards any TQM endeavors. Only if we can be assured that the organizational culture of say, a Macdonald's restaurant in Tokyo or in Beijing is exactly the same as that in its hometown in San Bernadino, California, then we can say that national cultures are less important than 'the' Macdonald's culture.

In proposing a theoretical framework for the culture-specific TQM, we build on the ARS theory of Anderson *et al.* (1994). It can be seen that the four inter-related propositions in the ARS theory represent the separate existence of TQM itself as a philosophy. Therefore, the result of transforming TQM into a culture-specific TQM or a hybrid system will depend on how the fusion effect works out with the particular culture in question. In other words, the ARS theory is modified to accommodate the important element of national culture as follow:

Proposition 1 (P1): The super-ordinate (national) cultural value system has an influence on the sub-value system (the organization) creating an organizational climate towards quality improvement (quality climate).
Proposition 2 (P2): The quality climate in turn determines or directs the processes of quality management (quality processes).
Proposition 3 (P3): The quality processes thus derived will lead to the implementation of certain specific quality activities (quality methods).
Proposition 4 (P4): The quality methods thus used will lead to consequences (quality results) to be enjoyed or suffered by the members of the organization.

These four inter-locking propositions represent a process-based theoretical framework for cultural influence on TQM. Its viability can thus be tested using actual data, which is the central activity of the present study. Taking into account the importance of quality culture, it is proposed in this theoretical framework that national culture does not directly affect the quality processes, quality methods, and quality results. The quality climate in the organization thus serves as an essential intermediary in articulating national culture into the concrete elements of TQM interventions. This argument is in line with the fusion effect proposition as stated previously. Clearly there may be commonalities or etic aspects among so-called American-style TQM, Japanese-style TQM, and Chinese-style TQM especially in terms of concrete elements such as certain quality processes and methods. Therefore, what is specific or

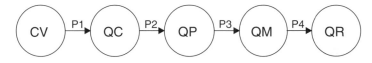

Figure 4.1   A process model of Chinese cultural values and TQM.

emic to the three TQM systems will be the kind of organizational climate pertaining to the culture-specific organization in question. As such, national cultural elements will be manifested in different ways among the three culture-specific systems.

A structural model of Chinese cultural values and TQM

From the previous discussion on Chinese cultural values, Confucianism does have an important place in Chinese societies today. The central theme of the study is therefore to find out the salient characteristics of the hybrid Chinese-style TQM when TQM itself is influenced by these important Confucian values. It is hoped that eventually a theoretical model explaining the associations among the constructs is generated. To this end, a number of steps were followed. In Chapter 2, the basic principles of TQM as known from the current literature were thoroughly reviewed. A suitable framework for TQM incorporating four quality variables namely: (1) climate (QC); (2) processes (QP); (3) methods (QM); and (4) results (QR) was proposed. Definitions of value and culture were presented and explained in Chapter 2. In Chapter 3, the characteristics and relevance of Chinese cultural values were discussed. These steps have led to the suggestion of a four-proposition theoretical framework for cultural influence on TQM in the present chapter. The four-proposition framework can now be depicted in the form of a simple structural model as shown in Figure 4.1.

In the structural model, the four-proposition framework is represented by the directional arrows P1, P2, P3, and P4. The variable CV represents Chinese cultural values exerting influences on the quality climate (QC) of the organization which in turn acts as an input element for quality processes (QP) and quality methods (QM). The result or output element of this model is represented by the quality results (QR). The entire model incorporating CV, QC, QP, QM, and QR therefore depicts a Chinese culture-specific TQM model. In the Chapter 5, the research methodology used in the present study is explained. Then, the structural model is operationalized and tested using empirical data.

5
Research Methodology

In this chapter, the samples and data gathering method are firstly identified and explained. Then, the origin and structure of the two research instruments employed in this empirical study are introduced. Finally, a structural equation model is devised to operationalize the culture-specific TQM as proposed in Chapter 4.

Samples and data collection method

This study employs samples of TQM companies operating in three Chinese regions namely, mainland China, Hong Kong, and Taiwan. However, due to the vast size of mainland China, most of the sampled companies included in this study were taken from the Guangdong province.

One methodological concern warrants special attention here. Hofstede (1980) stressed the importance of using 'matched samples' in cross-cultural research. Although, it is here virtually impossible to achieve such a close matching as what Hofstede did, the samples taken in this study are at least matched in terms of three characteristics. Firstly, all quality control managers who answered the questionnaires administered must be ethnic Chinese in companies not dominated by non-ethnic Chinese management. This assumes that all respondents have a similar background as to cultural values. Secondly, all sampled companies in this study have obtained ISO 9000 certifications, meaning that their quality management systems are basically similar. Thirdly, as at the time of actual data analysis, company certification history must be three years or more to assume that they have been practicing TQM to a certain degree. Although as stated in Chapter 2 that ISO 9000 should be considered only as a subset of TQM, choosing companies with ISO 9000 certification at least warrants that a certain level of quality management standard is achieved. Nevertheless, Iizuka's (1996) argument as discussed in Chapter 2 also provides support for the three-year criterion.

Data collection began in early 1997. For the case of Hong Kong, the author wrote to two major quality bodies in Hong Kong namely, the Hong Kong Quality Assurance Agency (HKQAA) and the Hong Kong Quality Management Association (HKQMA). The HKQAA is itself the largest ISO 9000 certification body in Hong Kong and a department of the semi-governmental Hong Kong productivity council. On the other hand, the HKQMA is a private association. A list containing 613 ISO 9000 certified companies in Hong Kong, in the form of a *Buyer's Guide July 1996*, was obtained from the HKQAA. A partial list of ISO 9000 companies was also obtained from the HKQMA. Upon comparison, information in this partial list was already fully covered in the *Buyer's Guide July 1996*. Thus the 613 ISO 9000 certified companies, covering 29 types of commercial activities including both manufacturing and service, formed the sampling frame for the region of Hong Kong.

For the case of mainland China, the author attempted to identify the population of all ISO 9000 companies operating in China through writing to the China State Bureau of Technical Standards in Beijing. Unfortunately, no centrally documented information could be obtained. The author thus relied on two main sources. Firstly, a database compiled in cooperation with researchers of a university in Southern China has located 253 ISO 9000 certified companies in the Guangdong province. Secondly, a list reported in the February 1997 issue of *China Quality* has included another 220 ISO 9000 certified companies scattered in 20 provinces and eight major cities in China. Though none of these two sources represented centrally compiled official information, the author decided to use the entire 473 companies as the sampling frame for China.

Concerning Taiwan, the author wrote to the Bureau of Commodity Inspection and Quarantine of the Ministry of Economic Affairs in Taiwan and obtained a list of 1200 ISO 9000 certified companies. This relatively large sampling frame for the region included companies scattered in the electric, electronic, mechanical, chemical, food, and service industries.

A set of questionnaires composing of two major research instruments was sent to each of the companies. The questionnaire administration period started in mid 1997 and lasted for around six months. A follow-up was conducted in February 1998. The final counts of valid returned questionnaires for mainland China, Hong Kong, and Taiwan were 117, 79, and 189 respectively, thus forming the sample of this study. The overall response rate was around 16.8 per cent. Nevertheless, according to

Malhotra (1993) and Yu and Cooper (1983), the response rate in a mailed survey without premailing contacts, prepaid or promised monetary or non-monetary incentives, and so on is typically less than 15 per cent.

Research instruments

The survey questionnaire used in this study is made up of two major research instruments namely, a modified version of the 'Quality and Productivity Self-Assessment Guide for Defense Organizations Version 1.0' (DoD, 1992) and the original version of the 'Chinese Cultural Value Scale' (Yau, 1994). They are now introduced in turn.

The TQM survey: origin and structure

In 1993, the Asian Productivity Organization (APO) launched a large-scale national survey on 'Quality Management Practices in Manufacturing and Service Sectors'. The objectives of the survey were to identify corporate needs through analyzing TQM practices and to enhance the capabilities for carrying them out in daily operations so as to improve business performance (Umeda, 1996: 4). Eleven members of the APO participated in the project. They included Bangladesh, Taiwan, Hong Kong, India, Indonesia, Islamic Republic of Iran, Republic of Korea, Nepal, the Philippines, Singapore, and Thailand. The national reports were subsequently published by APO in an edited volume entitled *TQM Practices in Asia-Pacific Firms* (Umeda, 1996).

The 'Quality and Productivity Self-Assessment Guide for Defense Organizations Version 1.0' (DoD, 1992) originally developed by the US Department of Defense was agreed to be used as the research instrument in the national survey. The country experts agreed on modifying the original instrument by reducing the number of questionnaire items from 215 to 73, covering most of the MBNQA examination criteria and the ISO 9001 standards. Also, for administering questionnaires, the length of the modified version is more appropriate as compared to using the original MBNQA or ISO 9000 criteria directly. The application of this instrument designed in the United States to Chinese companies should not give rise to pseudo-etic problems (Berry, 1969; Triandis and Marin, 1983; Yang, 1986) since it assesses the concrete management practices of the companies but not the personalities or values of the respondents.

The instrument has been adopted and denoted here as the TQM survey for convenience. The 73 items are assembled around four main quality variables as follows:

1. *Climate* (*items* 1–30): assessing the people's perceptions about the organization and/or the work unit. This dimension is renamed as QC in the present study.
2. *Processes* (*items* 31–57): assessing the organization's or work unit's policies, practices, and procedures. This dimension is renamed QP in the present study.
3. *Management tools* (*items* 58–63): assessing the specific techniques used to promote quality improvements throughout the organization or work unit. This dimension is renamed QM in the present study.
4. *Outcome* (*items* 64–73): assessing the organization's mission accomplishment. This dimension is renamed QR in the present study.

The wordings of the items were modified slightly by the author to allow for consistency so that all 73 questions were made to anchor on a 1 to 6 Likert-type scale covering: (1) strongly disagree; (2) disagree; (3) somehow disagree; (4) somehow agree; (5) agree; and (6) strongly agree. Since the TQM survey was to be administered to Chinese respondents in Hong Kong, China, and Taiwan, it was translated into Chinese by the author. To allow for translation, some wordings have been changed. The translation was checked by a university lecturer of Chinese studies. For objectivity and consistency, the author requested another lecturer to perform a back-translation (Brislin, 1980).

Since all sampled companies are ISO 9000 certified, it is important to ensure that the instrument covers most of the important ISO 9000 criteria. To allow for international standardization, the ISO 9001 standards were designed in a way that they are technically equivalent to the ANSI/ASQC Q90 series of quality system standards as adopted in the United States. On the other hand, these American standards form the foundation of the MBNQA criteria. In the United States, the MBNQA and the ISO 9000 certification are seen as mutually interconnected (Bureau of Business Practices, 1992: 115–20). Table 5.1 depicts the coverage of the MBNQA and the ISO 9001 criteria by the TQM survey.

Table 5.1 Coverage of the MBNQA examination criteria and the ISO 9001 by the TQM survey

	TQM survey item no.
MBNQA criteria	
1. Leadership	10, 11, 13, 15, 32, 33, 35, 62
2. Information and analysis	28, 30, 36, 43, 52, 53, 54

Table 5.1   (Continued)

	TQM survey item no.
3. Strategic quality planning	38, 39, 40, 42, 44, 45, 46, 63
4. Human resources development and management	1–9, 12, 16–21, 23, 29, 34, 41, 47, 48, 49, 51, 56, 57, 59, 61, 67
5. Management of process quality	22–26, 31, 50, 55, 58, 60, 69
6. Quality and operational results	64–66, 68, 70–72
7. Customer focus and satisfaction	14, 27, 37, 73, 74
ISO 9001 clauses	
4.1.1. Management responsibility – quality policy	1, 2, 5, 6, 7, 8, 10, 13, 18, 33, 38, 42, 43, 44, 45
4.1.2. Management responsibility – organization	16, 17, 19, 21, 23, 25, 32, 34, 35, 41, 46
4.1.3. Management responsibility – management review	28, 29, 49, 56
4.2. Quality system	3, 4, 13, 22, 33, 35, 39, 40, 42, 43, 44, 45, 59
4.3. Contract review	
4.4. Design control	70
4.5. Document and data control	36
4.6. Purchasing	20, 70
4.7. Control of customer supplied product	20, 70
4.8. Product identification and traceability	36
4.9. Process control	11, 12, 15, 31, 32, 41, 52, 53, 54, 55, 64
4.10. Inspection and testing	70, 71
4.11. Control of inspection, measuring, and test equipment	24, 66, 68
4.12. Inspection and test status	24, 66, 68
4.13. Control of non-conforming product	9, 15, 36, 71, 72, 73
4.14. Corrective action	9, 59, 71
4.15. Handling, storage, packaging, and delivery	65
4.16. Control of quality records	36
4.17. Internal quality audits	10, 11, 13, 14, 25, 31, 32, 36, 37, 39, 40, 41, 49, 52, 53, 54, 58, 59
4.18. Training	12, 26, 29, 30, 47, 48, 49, 50, 51, 56, 57, 61, 62, 63, 67, 69
4.19. Servicing	27, 72, 73
4.20. Statistical techniques	60

Source: Umeda (1996: 47, 54) adapted and expanded.

The CCV survey: origin and structure

The Chinese cultural values hypothesized to influence TQM in Chapter 4 are grounded on the dimensions derived form Yau's (1994) original findings. In his empirical research, an inventory of Chinese cultural values was developed to examine their relationships with consumer satisfaction in Hong Kong. A hundred common Chinese sayings were collected from various sources. After carefully considering expert opinions, the final version of the inventory was reduced to 45 items. Cronbach's α reliability coefficients obtained from two samples were above 0.8. Internal validity was assessed using the item-to-total correlation method (Cronbach and Meehl, 1955). All correlation coefficients were found to be significant at the 0.01 level. Furthermore, t-tests for each item of the scale across the two samples were not statistically significant showing that the instrument was internally consistent. In order to assess the external validity, the instrument was administered to two different groups, one Chinese and the other non-Chinese. A significant difference between the two groups existed at the 0.01 level, indicating that the instrument had reasonable external validity (Yau, 1994: 149–53). Factor analysis extracted 12 underlying Chinese cultural values which resembled those theoretical values anchored on Kluckhohn and Strodtbeck's (1961) value orientation framework as discussed in Chapter 3.

The original Chinese version of Yau's (1994) instrument, addressed here as CCV for convenience, was adopted in the present study. Although, published reports on the replication of the CCV are yet to be seen, there are several good reasons to adopt this instrument. Firstly, it is free from the problem of pseudo-etic application. Secondly, it carries simple everyday life sayings which every Chinese person can understand easily. It is expected that Chinese respondents should feel easier to express agreement or disagreement on a common saying rather than to a certain personal characteristic described by an adjective (cf. The Chinese Culture Connection, 1987; Cheung *et al.*, 1996). Furthermore, many value scales have been designed based on responses provided by university student samples for the sake of convenience. Yau (personal communication, 12 June 1997) strongly questioned the appropriateness of using student samples and any factor thus extracted should be dealt with care. The respondents of the present study had a closer resemblance to those who originally answered the CCV.

In the present study, the version administered to the Hong Kong and Taiwanese respondents were essentially the same. The mainland Chinese version was written in simplified Chinese characters. The respondents were asked to express their level of agreement or disagreement towards the 45 Chinese sayings using a Likert scale covering: (1) strongly disagree; (2) disagree; (3) somehow disagree; (4) somehow agree; (5) agree; and (6) strongly agree.

Before administering the research instruments to the sampled companies, a pilot test was firstly conducted. A convenience sample of 40 middle to lower level Chinese managers in Macau participated. They completed the questionnaires on their own and were asked to provide suggestions as to clarity and understandability. As a result, some wordings of the items in the TQM survey were slightly changed. Some participants even suggested that the six-point scale should be maintained so that no respondent would casually choose the median score. As to the CCV survey, no significant changes were suggested.

Structural equation model

Drawing from Jöreskog (1993: 295), structural equation modeling (SEM) can be employed under three different situations where the third one is the most common.

1. *Strictly confirmatory*: One single model has been formulated and is tested using empirical data so as to accept or reject it.
2. *Alternative models*: Several alternative or competing models have been formulated and one of them selected is given the best fit with a set of empirical data.
3. *Model generating*: A tentative initial model has been specified. A single set of data is used to test its fit. Driven by theory or data, the model is re-specified and tested again using the same data so that the model fits the data well from a statistical point of view. It is important also that every parameter of the model can be given a meaningful interpretation.

As the objective of the present study is mainly to generate a culture-specific TQM model through testing the four-proposition framework as developed in Chapter 4, a tentative structural model is developed. The approach follows the third one described by Jöreskog above. Based on prior review of existing theories, it possesses a confirmatory nature, but at the same time it serves also as a model generating process. Each of the four propositions is formulated into a testable hypothesis. This theoretical model is shown in the Figure 5.1.

In the model, Chinese cultural value (CV) is an independent variable while QC, QP, QM, and QR are dependent. The arrows represent influ-

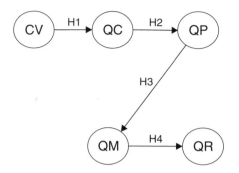

Figure 5.1 A structural model of Chinese cultural values and TQM.

ences or causal directions although causality must be carefully interpreted. They can be represented by the following hypotheses.

Hypothesis 1 (H1): There is a significant and positive association between CV and QC.
Hypothesis 2 (H2): There is a significant and positive association between QC and QP.
Hypothesis 3 (H3): There is a significant and positive association between QP and QM.
Hypothesis 4 (H4): There is a significant and positive association between QM and QR.

In testing the model, the SEM software AMOS 3.62 (Arbuckle, 1997) is used. The model is firstly formally specified in structural terms. The CV, QC, QP, QM, and QR are all treated as latent variables. Factors extracted from factor analysis are treated as observed variables for them. After all necessary data input procedures, the identification status of the model is established. The model is then subject to model fit evaluation based on absolute as well as adjunct fit indexes. All parameters represented in the hypotheses mentioned above can also be tested for statistical significance.

In order to verify the hypothesis that a culture-specific TQM system is influenced by national culture through an important intermediary namely, the QC of the organization, an alternative model as shown in Figure 5.2 is also suggested. In this alternative model, associations between CV and QP, CV and QM, and CV and QR are added. The following hypotheses are postulated in addition to H1 to H4 as proposed earlier.

Hypothesis 5 (H5): There is no significant association between CV and QP.

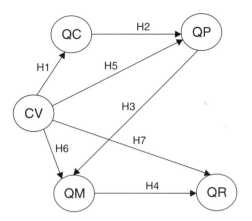

Figure 5.2   An alternative model of Chinese cultural values and TQM.

Hypothesis 6 (H6): There is no significant association between CV and QM.

Hypothesis 7 (H7): There is no significant association between CV and QR.

It is perhaps useful here to include a brief note on the controversial subject of causality. Early structural models were often known also as 'causal models' in the sense that they are able to demonstrate causalities among 'cause variables' and 'effect variables' in non-experimental research. However, there appear always difficulties in translating this deep philosophical issue into methodologies of the social sciences. Mueller's very vivid quote from Muthén (1992) is clear: 'For example, while some contemporary methodologists suggest that causal explanation is the ultimate aim of science, others insisted that it would be very healthy if more researchers abandon thinking of and using terms such as cause and effect' (Mueller, 1996: xii–xiii).

A faceted definition of causality was suggested by Mulaik (1987): 'Causality concerns the objective conception of the manner by which the variable properties of an object at a specified point in space and time determine unidirectionally by a functional relation the variable probabilistic, non-probabilistic properties of an object at a later point in space and time within a closed, self-contained system of interacting objects, defined in connection with a specific set of fixed background conditions'. In fact, this has long been challenged, for example, by the notion of a cause as a 'producing agent' (e.g. If X is a cause of Y, then a change in X produces a change in Y. This is a concept similar to that of 'forcing' known in science) making it difficult to translate the concept into logical or mathematical languages. Blalock argued that causal inferences belong to the theoretical level, whereas actual research can only establish covariation and temporal sequences. As a result, one can never actually demonstrate causal laws empirically. This is true even where experimentation is possible (Blalock, 1961: 172).

Mulaik and James (1995) stated that it is possible to fit models with different directions of causality to the same data and even achieve comparable fit. Similarly, Hoyle and Panter (1995: 175) pointed out that in many models, switching the direction of the association between two variables changes neither the overall fit of the model nor the parameter estimate of the association between the variables. In other words, SEM cannot overcome the limitations associated with non-experimental data gathered in a single session (Hoyle, 1995: 10).

Nevertheless, the SEM approach provides necessary but not sufficient conditions to establish causality. Blalock (1961: 14–15) stated that causal models should be thought of as containing desired simplifications. Although such models do not refer to reality, one can proceed by eliminating or modifying inadequate models that give predictions inconsistent with the data (pp. 20–2). Hoyle and Panter's advice seems most helpful and appropriate here. 'If the research methods and design that generated the data favor a causal inference, then such an inference can be made. Otherwise, the appropriate inference is that variables are reliably associated in the context of the model but the exact nature of the association cannot be demonstrated' (Hoyle and Panter, 1995: 175).

To conclude, establishing causality in structural models using non-experimental data is largely a matter of interpreting the research results with theoretical support and of course, common sense. Therefore, like the advice given by Hoyle and Panter above, a causal inference can be suggested if the research design is highly favorable towards such inference. When it comes to more complex questions in the social sciences, the same attitude should be held. Given the theoretical support for culture to be an influence on social behaviors, it is probably not too unreasonable to conclude that culture is one of many causes of certain social behaviors like for example, management practices although other cause elements must exist. The author is not trying to prove that Chinese cultural values 'cause' certain styles or status of quality management practices. Rather, the author wishes to identify an association between Chinese cultural values and quality management practices to support the fusion with the transcendent nature of TQM resulting in a Chinese culture-specific TQM model. If one prefers a more conservative perspective, one can interpret the result of the present study in terms of 'associations' rather than 'causes'.

Inputs for the structural models

Before the structural models are put to tests, reliability and validity of the input data have to be established. When a set of instrument items is designed to reflect an underlying construct, the items should be substantially correlated with one another. Also, for a given level of correlation among the measures, the greater the number of indicators, the more confidence we can have in the index constructed from them (Bohrnstedt and Knoke, 1988: 384). The Cronbach's α coefficient is a measure of the intercorrelation among the various indicators used to capture the underlying construct (Ghauri *et al.*, 1995: 47). Usually, a coefficient of 0.5 is regarded as reasonable in the social sciences. However, a stricter minimum value of 0.8 is usually preferred (Nunnally, 1978). It should be noted here that according to Bagozzi (1980; cited in Yau, 1994: 136), the Cronbach's α has the important property of being the lower bound for the reliability of a composite scale. Thus the actual reliability level could be somewhat higher than what is obtained from the coefficient.

To the degree that an operation results in observable measures that are accurate representations of a theory's concepts, the resulting measures are said to be valid (Bohrnstedt and Knoke, 1988: 12–13). Construct validity is perhaps the most crucial type of validity among all others. Lundstrom and Lamont (1976; cited in Yau, 1994: 137) suggested that construct validity can be assessed using the item-to-total correlation analysis. The item-to-total analysis works by comparing each individual item and the remaining items in the instrument. In other words, the correlation of each individual item score and the total score of the remaining items is computed and should be positive and statistically significant.

The entire sample of 385 observations is randomly divided into two sub-samples. The first sub-sample 1 of 190 observations is used for obtaining the underlying factors from the TQM survey and the CCV survey. The other sub-sample 2 of 195 observations is used for the model building process through structural equation modeling. In order to uncover the factors underlying the four dimensions (QC, QP, QM, and QR) of the TQM survey, exploratory factor analysis using principal component method is conducted in turn on each of these dimensions.

To interpret the meanings of the extracted factors, the extracted factors are subject to rotation. Orthogonal rotation has the advantage of eliminating multicolinearity among factors as well as improving the ease of factor interpretation. However, this rotation method usually assumes that underlying factors are not correlated, which is probably not the case here. Therefore, the promax oblique rotation is conducted instead. In analyzing the component items in a factor, factor loadings are usually considered. In the present study, items with loadings less than +0.5 are refrained from factor interpretation, and this threshold is considered to be very significant (Hair *et al.*, 1998: 111). Concerning the number of factors to be extracted, Kaiser's (1960; cited in Wood and Tataryn, 1996) 'eigenvalues-greater-than-one' rule is used only as a reference and not as an absolute rule. Wood and Tataryn (1996) pointed out that the Kaiser's criterion was found to be unsatisfactory in a number of studies. In any case, the author believes that it is more important to look at how meaningful the extracted factors are based on knowledge of existing literature and common sense. Therefore, the choice of factors from the TQM survey is determined based on the TQM framework elements as proposed in Chapter 2 rather than solely relying on quantitative indicators.

Since underlying Chinese cultural values have been identified already in Yau's (1994) empirical research, the objective now is to replicate those values and therefore confirmatory instead of exploratory factor analysis is appropriate. The attempt here is to confirm the structures of those 12 values as theoretically anchored on Kluckhohn and Strodtbeck's (1961) value orientation framework (Figure 3.1). To this end, the constituent scale items of those values namely, harmony with nature, *yuarn*, abasement, situation orientation, respect for authority, interdependence, group orientation, face, continuity, past time orientation, doctrine of the mean, and harmony with others need to be identified. This is achieved through scrutinizing the factor structures as reported in Yau's original findings and also carefully interpreting the literal meaning of each scale item. Sub-scale Cronbach's αs are then calculated. Due to the novelty of the CCV, αs within the range of 0.4–0.7 are expected. After the constituent items for each of the 12 values are identified, they are summated separately to obtain input scores for each value. Therefore, a confirmatory factor analysis model of a latent variable labeled CV (Chinese values) with 12 manifest variables each with a respective measurement error can be subject to test.

Based on the factor structures as derived from the processes described above, the entire structural equation model on the influence of Chinese cultural values on TQM can be devised. For this purpose, input scores calculated using sub-sample 2 with 195 observations will be used to fit the model. More details on model specification, estimation methods, and alternative models are provided in Chapter 6.

6
Data Analysis and Results

In this chapter, the profiles of the sampled companies are firstly introduced. Exploratory as well as confirmatory factor analyses are then conducted on the TQM and CCV surveys in order to uncover the underlying factors of quality climate, quality processes, quality methods, quality results, and Chinese cultural values. Finally, alternative models as suggested in Chapters 4 and 5 are postulated to test the proposed four-proposition framework so as to generate the culture-specific TQM model.

Characteristics of sampled companies

This section deals with an analysis of the background data of the respondent companies. The response rates, company size and type, and respondent profiles are depicted in Tables 6.1 to 6.5.

Table 6.1 Number of companies sampled and response rate

Region	No. of companies sampled	No. of companies in sampling frame and response rate in %
Hong Kong	79 (20.5%)	613 (12.9)
Taiwan	189 (49.1%)	1200 (15.8)
China	117 (30.4%)	473 (24.7)
Total	385 (100%)	2286 (16.8)

Table 6.2   Sampled companies by size, type, and type in detail

	No. of companies	%
Company size		
Over 200 employees	228	59.2
Less than 200 employees	144	37.4
Unknown	13	3.4
Total	385	100
Company type		
Manufacturing	342	88.8
Service	42	10.9
Unknown	1	0.3
Total	385	100
Company type (detailed)		
1. Manufacturing	288	74.8
2. Retail or wholesale	8	2.1
3. Construction	52	13.5
4. Transport and communication	12	3.1
5. Financial services	2	0.5
6. Professional services	20	5.2
7. Others	2	0.5
8. Unknown	1	0.3
Total	385	100

Note: Types 1 and 3 were classified under 'manufacturing'. Types 2, 4, 5, and 6 were under 'service'.

Table 6.3   Sampled companies by type and size (region specific)

	Hong Kong		Taiwan		Mainland China	
	No. of Companies	%	No. of Companies	%	No. of Companies	%
Company type						
Manufacturing	49	62.0	186	98.4	107	91.5
Service	29	36.7	3	1.6	10	8.5
Unknown	1	1.3	–	–	–	–
Total	79	100	189	100	117	100
Company size						
Over 200 employees	36	45.6	99	52.4	93	79.5

Less than 200 employees	41	51.9	88	46.6	15	12.8
Unknown	2	2.5	2	1.1	9	7.7
Total	79	100	189	100	117	100

Table 6.4 Respondents by sex, age brackets, and job positions

	No. of respondents	%
Respondents' sex		
Male	278	72.2
Female	61	15.8
Unknown	44	11.9
Total	385	100
Age bracket		
Less than 20	1	0.3
20–30	67	17.4
31–40	130	33.8
41–50	98	25.5
51–60	26	6.8
Over 60	4	1.0
Unknown	59	15.3
Total	385	100
Job position		
Company director	58	15.1
Quality control engineer	102	26.5
ISO 9000 director	12	3.1
Plant manager	134	34.8
Unknown	79	20.5
Total	385	100

Table 6.5 Characteristics of two randomly split sub-samples

	Sub-sample 1		Sub-sample 2	
	No. of observations	%	No. of observations	%
In terms of region				
Hong Kong	42	22.1	37	19.0
Taiwan	94	49.5	95	48.7
China	54	28.4	63	32.3
Total	190	100	195	100

Table 6.5   (Continued)

	Sub-sample 1		Sub-sample 2	
	No. of observations	%	No. of observations	%
In terms of company size				
Large (over 200 employees)	101	53.2	127	65.1
Small (less than 200 employees)	81	42.6	63	32.3
Unknown	8	4.2	5	2.6
Total	190	100	195	100
In terms of company type				
Manufacturing	162	85.3	180	92.3
Service	27	14.2	15	7.7
Unknown	1	0.5	–	–
Total	190	100	195	100

Exploratory factor analysis on the TQM survey

In this section, exploratory factor analysis is conducted on the TQM survey. Factor analysis helps to identify the dimensions and their structure of relationships which are not directly observable from a much larger set of variables for use in subsequent multivariate analyses (Hair *et al.*, 1998: 95). Usually, the reduced variables provide better data normality and homogeneity of variance and covariance. In the present instance, the TQM survey is itself divided into four sections namely, QC, QP, QM, and QR. Four factor analyses have to be conducted in order to reveal the factors corresponding to each of these four sections. Since factor analyses are to be conducted, sub-scale reliability coefficients (Cronbach's α of extracted factors to each of the four dimensions) will be reported afterwards.

In order to assess the validity of the survey, the item-to-total correlation method as described in Chapter 5 is employed. Again, if the instrument was valid, with all items measuring the same concept, the product-moment correlation of each item to the total of the remaining items should be positive and statistically significant. Based on the aggregate of all the three regional samples, the item-to-total correlation coefficients are separately calculated for the four dimensions of the survey. Correlation coefficients obtained from the QC, QP, QM, and QR items ranged from 0.48 to 0.73, 0.61 to 0.82, 0.69 to 0.78, and 0.51 to 0.75 respectively. All of them are positive and statistically significant at $p = 0.000$.

Before performing the factor analysis, it is vital that the assumptions underlying this statistical method be met. According to Hair *et al.* (1998: 98–9), a general rule is to have at least five times as many observations as there are variables to be analyzed. In the present research, the total sample size in sub-sample 1 is 190, number of items in the QC, QP, QM, and QR sections are 30, 27, 6, and 10 respectively. The sample size requirement is met. Furthermore, any departures from normality, homoscedasticity, and linearity apply only to the extent that they diminish the observed correlation and in fact some degree of multi-colinearity is desirable (p. 99). Normality tests on the 73 individual items univariately show significant ($p = 0.000$) Kolmogorov-Smirnov Lilliefors adjusted statistics in many of them. Skewness range from −0.209 to −1.322 and kurtosis from −0.071 to 2.299. However, this departure from normality should not create substantial problems for the factor analytic procedures.

The popular method of principal component analysis is used. It is especially appropriate when one wishes to predict the minimum number of factors needed to account for the maximum portion of variances in the original variables (Hair *et al.*, 1998: 102). Also, this method works best when the original variables are very highly correlated (Manly, 1986: 60), which is the present case. As explained in Chapter 5, the Kaiser's eigenvalue-greater-than-one criterion for factor extraction may not always provide the appropriate number of factors to be extracted. Prior understanding of the instrument and theoretical considerations are of great importance for effective factor extraction. Finally, since the Bartlett test of sphericity indicates that the factors are highly inter-correlated, they are rotated using the promax oblique rotation method.

Table 6.6 shows the results of four principal component factor analyses, each performed on the QC, QP, QM, and QR items respectively. The percentages of variances of the original variables accounted for by the extracted factors are also shown in the table. A higher value (maximum one) for the Kaiser-Myer-Olkin (KMO) test for sampling adequacy indicates a higher suitability of using factor analysis. A significant Bartlett statistic indicates that the original variables are correlated.

Table 6.7 summarizes the 11 factors obtained from the four factor analyses. Sub-scale Cronbach's α reliability coefficients calculated using 195 observations from sub-sample 2 are also provided. By examining the items and considering their loadings, the factors are given appropriate

Table 6.6　Eigenvalues of extracted factors of QC, QP, QM, and QR items

Factors	Eigenvalue	% variance explained	Cumulative % of variance explained
QC factors			
Factor 1	13.637	45.458	45.458
Factor 2	1.934	6.446	51.904
Factor 3	1.645	5.482	57.386
Factor 4	1.103	3.675	61.062
			KMO = 0.935
			Bartlett = 3703 (df = 435, p = 0.000)
QP factors			
Factor 5	15.651	57.968	57.968
Factor 6	1.239	4.589	62.557
Factor 7	1.025	3.796	66.353
			KMO = 0.957
			Bartlett = 4275 (df = 351, p = 0.000)
QM factors			
Factor 8	4.104	68.404	68.404
Factor 9	0.560	9.342	77.745
			KMO = 0.877
			Bartlett = 698 (df = 15, p = 0.000)
QR factors			
Factor 10	5.235	52.351	52.351
Factor 11	0.958	9.578	61.928
			KMO = 0.903
			Bartlett = 912 (df = 45, p = 0.000)

Table 6.7　Eleven factors extracted from the TQM survey

Instrument items	Factors extracted
Quality climate (QC) Sub-scale α = 0.834	Factor 1: Commitment to quality Factor 2: Unity of purpose Factor 3: Harmonious system Factor 4: Communication
Quality processes (QP) Sub-scale α = 0.880	Factor 5: Organizational planning and evaluation Factor 6: Organizational flexibility and employee orientation Factor 7: Training and information analysis
Quality methods (QM) Sub-scale α = 0.801	Factor 8: Teamwork Factor 9: Scientific approach
Quality results (QR) Sub-scale α = 0.847	Factor 10: Customer satisfaction Factor 11: Workplace *kaizen*

names. The 11 factors obtained are quite consistent with those common TQM elements surveyed from the various writers as discussed in Chapter 2. Tables 6.8 to 6.11 depict the factor structures and their loadings. Loadings less than 0.5 are suppressed.

Table 6.8 Four factors and item loadings of QC

	Loading
Factor 1: Commitment to quality	
The supervisors in my work unit regularly ask our customers about the quality of work they receive	0.837
The way we do things in this organization is consistent with quality	0.830
People in my work unit believe that quality and productivity improvement is their responsibility	0.813
People in my work unit understand how a quality emphasis leads to more productive use of resources	0.810
Every member of this organization is concerned with the need for quality	0.763
The supervisors in my work unit make the continuous improvement of our work top priority	0.745
People in this organization emphasize doing things right the first time	0.733
People in my work unit believe that their work is important to the success of the overall organization	0.687
Creativity is actively encouraged in this organization	0.637
Factor 2: Unity of purpose	
People in this organization are aware of its overall mission	0.862
People in this organization are aware of how the organization's mission contribute to higher-level missions and objectives	0.860
People in this organization try to plan ahead for changes that might impact our mission performance	0.726
People in this organization regularly work together to plan for the future	0.718
People in this organization see continuing improvement as essential	0.570
Every member of this organization knows how to define the quality of what we do	0.523
Factor 3: Harmonious system	
We have the right tools, equipment, and materials in my work unit to get the job done	0.778
Attempts are made to promote the people in my work unit who do good work	0.708
My work unit is structured properly to get the job done	0.538
People in my work unit care about our customers	0.505

Table 6.8   (Continued)

	Loading
Factor 4: Communication	
People in my work unit have ample opportunity to exchange information with their supervisors	0.756
People in my work unit get the facts and the information they need to do a good job	0.657
People in my work unit enjoy their co-workers	0.652
People in my work unit know how their supervisors will help them find answers to problems they may be having	0.641

Table 6.9   Three factors and item loadings of QP

	Loading
Factor 5: Organizational planning and evaluation	
The leaders at the top level in this organization have set long-term goals concerning quality improvement	0.893
All work units within this organization have defined performance measures to monitor progress towards reaching their objectives and goals	0.844
The leaders at the top level in this organization have defined performance measures to monitor progress towards reaching objectives and goals	0.823
This organization has quality improvement policy that has specific goals and objectives	0.777
This organization has analyzed data concerning goal/objective accomplishments in order to determine whether improvements in quality are needed	0.706
Managers at all levels have clearly defined roles in our quality improvement process	0.704
In order to determine what our customers think about our products/services/work, we conduct surveys on a regular basis	0.695
Responsibility for quality performance improvement is accepted by almost all organizational members	0.640
Long-range planning in this organization includes prioritizing quality improvement issues	0.629
This organization is (or might become) committed to quality improvement because we want to improve an already acceptable quality record	0.533
In order to tell how well we are doing as an organization, we monitor data about the quality of our services/products/work	0.508
Factor 6: Organizational flexibility and employee orientation	
Top-performing managers at all levels in this organization can expect increased responsibility	0.896

In terms of setting organizational improvement priorities, we have considered or evaluated improving our work methods or procedures	0.774
The performance appraisals of organizational members include quality improvement criteria	0.715
In terms of setting organizational improvement priorities, we have considered or evaluated changing our business strategy	0.706
Organizational members are informed about how this work unit stands in relation to goals, objectives, or standards	0.670
The future strength of this organization depends on the continuing growth of its members through appropriate training	0.666
Organizational members with good ideas are likely to formally submit them through a suggestion system	0.665
This organization has used teams to gather information or solve problems	0.656
The performance data that this organization collects are compared with goals, standards, or objectives	0.618
The performance data that this organization collects are used to identify opportunities for quality improvement	0.544
Factor 7: Training and information analysis	
Organizational members have been adequately trained to use the equipment they have	0.883
The organization has a database or tracking system for relevant quality information	0.575
People in charge of similar work units frequently share information about their work methods and practices	0.572
The structure of this organization supports its efforts to carry out its missions	0.528

Table 6.10 Two factors and item loadings of QM

	Loading
Factor 8: Teamwork	
This organization has attempted to inform and involve everyone in quality improvement	0.961
This organization has established improvement teams (groups of individuals who come together to solve quality-related problems)	0.926
This organization has arranged workshops to promote quality awareness among its members	0.674
This organization has called groups of individuals together to define performance measures to track progress toward goal attainment	0.545

Table 6.10   (Continued)

	Loading
Factor 9: Scientific approach	
This organization has used statistical process control charts or graphs to track data over time	0.788
This organization has used surveys to assess quality of its work	0.647

Table 6.11   Two factors and item loadings of QR

	Loading
Factor 10: Customer satisfaction	
The organizational customers find minimal errors in our work	0.950
The organizational customers are satisfied with the quality of our work	0.853
Organizational members rarely need to redo a job or task	0.840
This organization's materials and supplies meet quality specifications	0.724
Factor 11: Workplace kaizen	
The personnel turnover is low	0.854
Tools and/or equipment are maintained and operated at peak efficiency	0.819
Once a job or project gets started, it is usually finished without undue delay	0.752
People make effort to reuse or salvage excess materials and supplies whenever possible	0.616
Organizational members receive the guidance and assistance they need to accomplish their work	0.518

Confirmatory factor analysis on the CCV survey

After the factors underlying the TQM survey have been extracted, the CCV survey is now subject to a data reduction process. The objective here is to identify the factor structure of the 12 Chinese cultural values (harmony with nature, *yuarn*, abasement, situation orientation, respect for authority, interdependence, group orientation, face, continuity, past time orientation, doctrine of the mean, and harmony with others) which have been theoretically anchored on Kluckhohn and Strodtbeck's (1961) value orientation framework described in Chapter 3. For this purpose, confirmatory factor analysis is more appropriate since we already have *a priori* factor structures as given in Yau's (1994) original study. Table 6.12 provides the final factor structure of 11 Chinese cultural values (interdependence and group orientation have been combined as one value due to their similarity). The structural items are finalized by carefully scrutinizing Yau's original factor items as well as thoroughly reviewing their Chinese literal meanings. In an iterative manner, items are added together or dropped and Cronbach's α reliability coefficient calculated and recalculated. In any case, the objective is to strike a balance between qualitative (convergence of literal meanings) and quantitative (reliability coefficient) concerns.

Table 6.12   Factor structures of 11 Chinese cultural values

Value 1. Harmony with nature ($\alpha = 0.737$)
Live as it is predestined.
He who submits to Heaven shall live; he who rebels against Heaven shall perish.
Do all that is humanly possible and leave the rest to the will of providence.
Life and death are fated; wealth and honors hinge on the will of providence.
Fate is predestined.

Value 2. Yuarn
At a different time and in a different place we will meet again.

Value 3. Abasement ($\alpha = 0.679$)
Haughtiness invites ruin; humility receives benefits.
Reflect on our faults when we take a rest.
Endure and you will find everything all right; retreat and you will find yourself happy.
Beyond a mountain, yet a higher one.
If we want to criticize others, criticize ourselves first.
Never forget what others have done for you.
Face is honored by others; shame is sought by ourselves.

Value 4. Situation orientation ($\alpha = 0.530$)
When in Rome, do as the Romans do.
Blessing abound in a family that preserves in good deeds.
A family has its rules as a state has its laws.
Those against the laws should be punished.
A man who can survive in hardship is the man of men.
Better bend than break.

Value 5. Respect for authority ($\alpha = 0.669$)
Children should report everything to their parents.
Reject an old man's advice and you'll soon pay for it.
I will treat my teacher as my father even though he has taught me for one day.
Children have to respect the decisions of their parents.
Live with your parents after marriage.
Old parents are just like treasure in your house when living with.

Table 6.12   (Continued)

Value 6. Group orientation/Interdependence ($\alpha = 0.692$)
Forgive others whenever you can.
A man depends on his parents at home.
Help each other whenever in need.
Never forget what others have done for you.
A family will be prosperous if it is in harmony.
Blessing abound in a family that preserves in good deeds.
A family has its rules as a state has its laws.
If you honor me a linear foot, I should in return honor you ten feet.

Value 7. Face ($\alpha = 0.587$)
Shameful affairs of the family should not be spoken outside.
It is more urgent to pay back favors than debts.
Face is honored by others; shame is sought by ourselves.
If you honor me a linear foot, I should in return honor you ten feet.
Forgive others whenever you can.

Value 8. Continuity ($\alpha = 0.460$)
To have a son for old age is to stock provision for a rainy day.
Of the three practices of unfilial piety, having no son is the greatest.

Value 9. Past time orientation
The new generation is worse than the old.

Value 10. Doctrine of the mean
No matter what you are doing, don't go too far.

Value 11. Harmony with others ($\alpha = 0.653$)
I won't offend others unless I am offended.
An eye for an eye.
There is deceit in excessive courtesy.
To please someone without a cause is either adulterous or greedy.
I will return favors and take revenge as well.

As can be seen from Table 6.12, harmony with nature, abasement, respect for authority, interdependence/group orientation, and harmony with others have rather acceptable Cronbach's αs ranging from 0.65 to 0.74. Situation orientation, face, and continuity show weaker αs ranging from a minimally acceptable 0.45 to 0.59. Due to the original design of the CCV survey, *yuarn*, past time orientation, and doctrine of the mean are only represented by single surrogate measures and may not be so stable. Psychometrically speaking, the CCV survey as a novel value scale does possess certain weaknesses. Nevertheless, the subsequent confirmatry factor analysis can better assess the veracity of these 11 factors on the single latent construct of Chinese cultural values. For further analysis, items loaded on a factor or value are aggregated and the summated scores calculated (Hair *et al.*, 1998).

Normality tests on the 11 values show that only harmony with nature is normally distributed at the 0.05 level (Kolmogorov-Smirnov Lilliefors adjusted statistic 0.64, $p = 0.054$). Normality statistics for all the other ten values show significant non-normality ($p = 0.000$). For the purpose of confirmatory factor analysis and structural equation modeling, some statistical problems may arise when normality is violated although some researchers have reckoned that normal theory estimation methods such as generalized least square (GLS) and in some cases maximum likelihood (ML) are found to be less sensitive to non-normality (Browne and Shapiro, 1988; Amemiya and Anderson, 1990; Satorra and Bentler, 1990, 1991; Hu and Bentler, 1995; Schumacker and Lomax, 1996). Generally speaking, when the normality assumption is violated, normal theory ML and GLS produce χ^2 values which are too large especially when sample size is small. Also, standard errors as well as some fit indices such as the Tucker-Lewis index (TLI) and the comparative fit index (CFI) are also underestimated (West *et al.*, 1995: 62–3). In order to deal with the problem, Browne's (1984) asymptotic distribution free (ADF) method which does not rely on the normality assumption can be used. However, this method usually requires a sample size of at least 1000 for simple models and around 5000 for complex models in order to provide unbiased estimates (West *et al.*, 1995: 68).

Other methods which can be used to minimize the discrepancy function such as scale free least square (SLS) or unweighted least square (ULS) are not known to rest on any distributional assumptions. However, these methods are unable to estimate standard errors and thus the statistical significance of parameters. Fortunately, with the availability of modern computing facilities, bootstrapping (Efron and Tibshirani, 1986) serves as an effective remedy. Empirical sampling distributions taken from bootstrap samples can often be reasonably approximated based on a single sample. Thus, by taking a large number of bootstrap samples from the original sample, the mean and variance of the empirical bootstrap sampling distribution can be approximated (West *et al.*, 1995: 66).

Another characteristic of the SLS or ULS method is that no χ^2 statistic is produced as in normal theory ML or GLS. Therefore, one cannot deterministically evaluate whether the entire model is accepted or not at a certain level of statistical significance. In fact, the χ^2 hypothesis testing technique is affected by many factors such as sample size and model complexity (Cochran, 1952; Gulliksen and Tukey, 1958; Jöreskog, 1969; Bentler and Bonett, 1980). As stated by Kaplan (1995: 101), models never fit data perfectly and will always contain specification errors which are often magnified by larger sample sizes and masked by smaller sample sizes. Therefore, normal theory ML or GLS tend to favor a smaller sample size and will therefore produce a non-significant χ^2 value. On the other hand, when the sample size is large, the χ^2 value produced will inevitably be significant and therefore the model always rejected. Thus, instead of relying on χ^2 hypothesis testing, it is actually more meaningful to put the hypothesized model into some perspective. For example, goodness of fit indices of the model can be compared with those of 'baseline' cases (models with the worst possible fit) such as the independence model or the zero model in order to evaluate the veracity of the hypothesized covariance structure. Due to non-normality of the variables involved, all confirmatory factor analyses and structural equation models in the present study are estimated using SLS with bootstrapping procedures.

To perform a confirmatory factor analysis on the 11 variables as measures of Chinese cultural values, the measurement model as presented in Figure 6.1 is used. Chinese cultural values (CV) is a latent variable which is explained by 11 manifest variables namely, harmony with nature (V1), *yuarn* (V2), abasement (V3), situation orientation (V4), respect for authority (V5), group orientation/interdependence (V6), face (V7), continuity (V8), past time orientation (V9), doctrine of the mean (V10), and harmony with others (V11). Each manifest variable is associated with a measurement error (e12 to e17). Conventionally, certain parameters are fixed at unity to allow for model identification. From sub-sample 1, 190 observations are used.

Using SLS estimation, a minimum discrepancy function of 119.869 is obtained. Compared to that of the independence model (1107.485) or the zero model (2146.985), the model shows an acceptable level of fit. Goodness-of-fit index (GFI) and adjusted goodness-of-fit index (AGFI) show 0.944 and 0.916 respectively (independence model GFI 0.484, AGFI 0.381). By taking 1000 bootstrap samples, approximate parameter estimates and their corresponding standard errors are obtained. Statistical significance can thus be established by calculating critical values for each parameter estimate. All regression weights and variances are significant at the 0.05 level (critical ratios larger than 1.96) except CV → V9 (past time orientation). All bootstrap estimated square multiple correlation coefficients indicate reasonable construct validity except V9 (V1 0.214, V2 0.181, V3 0.557, V4 0.470, V5 0.319, V6 0.669, V7 0.542, V8 0.145, V9 0.016, V10 0.170, V11 0.185). Using only one single surrogate measure to measure time orientation is an inherent weakness of the original CCV

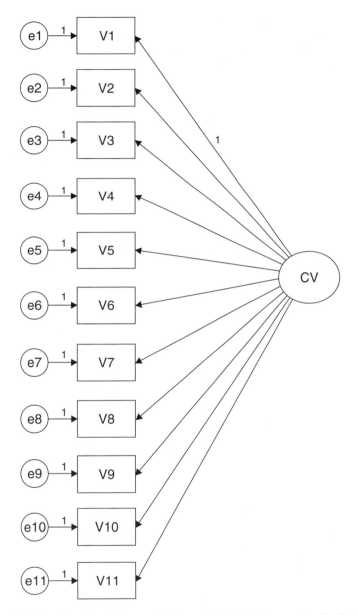

Figure 6.1 Confirmatory factor analysis model of 11 Chinese cultural values.

Note: harmony with nature (V1), *yuarn* (V2), abasement (V3), situation orientation (V4), respect for authority (V5), group orientation/interdependence (V6), face (V7), continuity (V8), past time orientation (V9), doctrine of the mean (V10), and harmony with others (V11).

Table 6.13   Unstandardized output of Chinese cultural value model

Parameter	Bootstrap estimate	Bootstrap standard error	Bootstrap critical ratio
CV→V1	1.000		
CV→V2	0.173	0.048	3.604
CV→V3	1.330	0.284	4.683
CV→V4	1.019	0.185	5.508
CV→V5	1.332	0.280	4.757
CV→V6	1.518	0.308	4.928
CV→V7	1.040	0.217	4.792
CV→V8	0.381	0.103	3.699
CV→V9	0.062	0.058	1.069*
CV→V10	0.155	0.044	3.523
CV→V11	0.736	0.147	5.007
CV	4.625	1.524	3.035
E1	16.885	2.108	8.010
E2	0.586	0.061	9.607
E3	5.924	0.686	8.636
E4	5.009	0.672	7.453
E5	16.456	2.072	7.942
E6	4.805	0.827	5.810
E7	3.859	0.531	7.267
E8	3.869	0.386	10.023
E9	1.933	0.163	11.859
E10	0.501	0.068	7.368
E11	10.663	1.329	8.023

*$p > 0.05$

survey design. When V9 is dropped from the analysis, the discrepancy function is significantly reduced to 90.138. GFI and AGFI increase to 0.955 and 0.930. Nevertheless, considering the entirety of Kluckhohn and Strodtbeck's (1961) five dimensional value orientation framework, V9 is retained in the present instance. Inclusion of multiple indicators for past time orientation, *yuarn*, and doctrine of the mean is called for in future redesign of the scale. Details of the output model are carried in Table 6.13. The standardized output model is depicted in Figure 6.2.

Hypothesized model of Chinese cultural values on TQM

In this section, the hypothesized model of Chinese cultural values affecting a four-variable quality management framework is tested. The theoretical propositions developed in Chapter 4 are restated as follows.

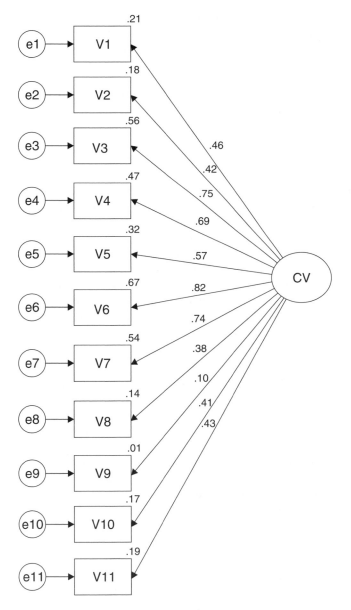

Figure 6.2 Standardized output of Chinese cultural value model.

Note: harmony with nature (V1), *yuarn* (V2), abasement (V3), situation orientation (V4), respect for authority (V5), group orientation/interdependence (V6), face (V7), continuity (V8), past time orientation (V9), doctrine of the mean (V10) and harmony with others (V11).

Proposition 1: The super-ordinate (national) cultural value system has an influence on the sub-value system (the organization) creating an organizational climate towards quality improvement (quality climate).

Proposition 2: The quality climate in turn determines or directs the processes of quality management (quality processes).

Proposition 3: The quality processes thus derived will lead to the implementation of certain specific quality activities (quality methods).

Proposition 4: The quality methods thus used will lead to consequences (quality results) to be enjoyed or suffered by the members of the organization.

These propositions can now be operationalized into testable hypotheses (H1, H2, H3, and H4) through devising a structural equation model. Before testing the hypothesized model as shown in Figure 6.3, a brief review of its components is given here. For convenience, this model is denoted as the full model since an alternative model will be tested in subsequent sections. The constituents of the full model are firstly reviewed. CV is a latent variable representing Chinese cultural values. It is measured by 11 observable or manifest variables namely, harmony with nature (V1), *yuarn* (V2), abasement (V3), situation orientation (V4), respect for authority (V5), group orientation/interdependence (V6), face (V7), continuity (V8), past time orientation (V9), doctrine of the mean (V10), and harmony with others (V11). This 11-factor model has been validated through confirmatory factor analysis in the last section.

The other major part of the full model is the four-variable quality management framework. It has four main components namely: (1) quality climate (QC); (2) quality processes (QP); (3) quality methods (QM); and (4) quality results (QR), each being treated as a latent construct. Manifest variables for each of them have been identified through factor analyses. They include commitment to quality (F1), unity of purpose (F2), harmonious system (F3), and communication (F4) for QC. Organizational planning and evaluation (F5), organizational flexibility and employee orientation (F6), and training and information analysis (F7) for QP. Teamwork (F8) and scientific approach (F9) for QM. Customer satisfaction (F10) and workplace *kaizen* (F11) for QR.

The regression path between CV and QC (H1) represents the impact of Chinese cultural values on the companies' organizational climate. As stated in Chapter 2, cultural values at the macro level are exemplified at the micro level in terms of organizational climate. This in turn influences the processes and results of the organization. In other words, QC acts as an intermediary between CV and the other quality variables namely, QP,

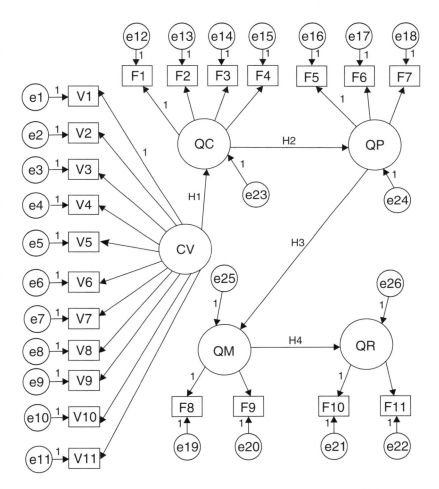

Figure 6.3 Hypothesized full model of Chinese cultural values on TQM.

QM, and QR. The full model is tested using the SLS estimation method with 1000 bootstrap samples to generate robust parameter estimates.

Using SLS estimation, a minimized discrepancy function of 250.091 is obtained. Comparing to that of the independence model (6333.496) or the zero model (8467.496), the suggested model shows a reasonably acceptable fit. Goodness-of-fit index and AGFI are 0.970 and 0.964 respectively (independence model GFI 0.252, AGFI 0.181). Other fit indices such as the norm-fit index (NFI) and relative-fit index (RFI) show satisfactory fit at 0.961 and 0.956 respectively. The path CV → V9 is again non-significant at the 0.05 level as in the confirmatory factor analysis model conducted in the last section. In addition, path CV → V11 is also non-significant. This indicates that further research on the construct validity of CV in terms of some of the underlying values is warranted. If these two paths were dropped from the analysis, the minimum discrepancy function would reduce to 166.414; GFI, AGFI, NFI, and RFI would increase to 0.980, 0.974, 0.973, and 0.969 respectively.

Apart from the two non-significant paths, all other regression paths are in their intended directions and are significant at the 0.05 level. Basically there are not serious problems sufficient to judge the model to

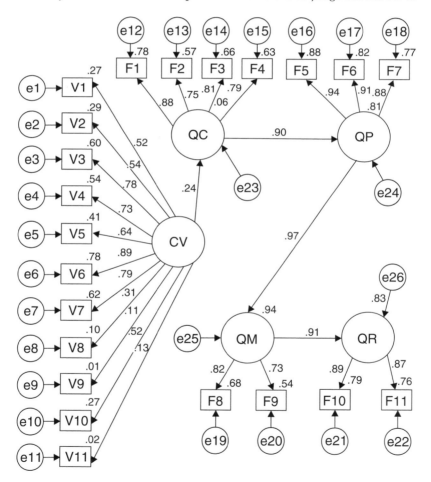

Figure 6.4   Standardized output of full model.

be wrong. In terms of explanatory power of individual dependent variables, the bootstrap estimated square multiple correlation coefficients of QC, QP, QM, and QR are 0.073, 0.817, 0.934, and 0.831 respectively. As expected, the impact of CV on QC is not exceptionally high because the two variables are of very different nature. The former belongs to an abstract human cultural phenomenon while the latter is a more concrete organizational situation. Nevertheless, Bohrnstedt and Knoke (1988: 236) have pointed out that typically a single independent variable in the social sciences will often account for as little as five to ten per cent the variance in a dependent variable. On the other hand, since QC, QP, QM, and QR belong to a concrete and closely interlocking TQM framework, it is expected that the percentages of variance explained should be very high as in the case. Given the satisfactory overall fit of the model, the hypothesized structure is nonetheless a feasible model representing the influence of Chinese cultural values on TQM. Details of the parameter estimates are carried in Table 6.14. The standardized output model is shown in Figure 6.4.

Table 6.14   Unstandardized bootstrap output of hypothesized full model

Path	Mean	Standard error	Critical ratio	Variance	Mean	Standard error	Critical ratio
QC←CV	0.697	0.319	2.185	E1	14.007	1.751	7.999
QP←QC	1.251	0.089	14.056	E2	0.522	0.077	6.779
QM←QP	0.366	0.025	14.640	E3	5.183	0.948	5.467
QR←QM	0.848	0.078	10.872	E4	4.356	0.652	6.681
F1←QC	1.000			E5	13.585	1.740	7.807
F2←QC	0.595	0.050	11.900	E6	3.743	0.838	4.467
F3←QC	0.409	0.032	12.781	E7	2.824	0.489	5.775
F4←QC	0.400	0.038	10.526	E8	3.395	0.353	9.618
F5←QP	1.000			E9	1.864	0.153	12.183
F6← QP	0.834	0.031	26.903	E10	0.557	0.075	7.427
F7←QM	0.351	0.016	21.938	E11	11.276	1.645	6.855
F8 ←QM	1.000			E12	10.213	2.586	3.949
F9 ←QR	0.504	0.032	15.750	E13	9.444	1.633	5.783
F10←QR	1.000			E14	3.172	0.555	5.715
F11←QR	1.373	0.088	15.602	E15	3.419	0.498	6.866
V1←CV	1.000			E16	8.853	2.037	4.346
V2←CV	0.212	0.053	4.000	E17	10.110	1.920	5.266
V3←CV	1.292	0.284	4.550	E18	2.494	0.584	4.271
V4←CV	1.045	0.235	4.447	E19	4.651	0.724	6.424
V5←CV	1.389	0.245	5.669	E20	2.102	0.309	6.803
V6←CV	1.647	0.321	5.131	E21	2.155	0.507	4.251
V7←CV	0.990	0.181	5.470	E22	4.964	1.099	4.517
V8←CV	0.265	0.071	3.732	E23	33.379	6.333	5.271

Table 6.14   (Continued)

Path	Mean	Standard error	Critical ratio	Variance	Mean	Standard error	Critical ratio
V9←CV	0.062	0.052	1.192*	E24	12.453	3.437	3.623
V10←CV	0.209	0.048	4.354	E25	0.623	0.534	1.167*
V11←CV	0.200	0.149	1.342*	E26	1.401	0.495	2.830
				CV	5.256	1.836	2.863

*$p > 0.05$

Alternative model of Chinese cultural values on TQM

An alternative model is postulated to test the importance of organizational climate being an intermediary between Chinese cultural values and the other quality variables. The hypothesis raised is that if QC is not important as an intermediary, then CV can directly, positively, and significantly affect the remaining quality variables namely, QP, QM, and QR. Thus the original full model is now modified to include three new regression paths labeled H5, H6, and H7 from CV to QP, QM, and QR respectively as shown in Figure 6.5. H5, H6, and H7 also represent the three additional hypotheses as raised in Chapter 5.

Using SLS estimation with 1000 bootstrap samples again, the minimized discrepancy function and the various fit indices do not vary too much from those obtained in the full model. Nevertheless, this does not point to the conclusion that the alternative model is correct. The newly added regression paths are of interest here. Firstly, the bootstrap estimated regression paths of QC ← CV, QP ← QC, QM ← QP, and QR ← QM are 0.748 (standard error = 0.300, critical ratio = 2.493), 1.282 (standard error = 0.098, critical ratio = 13.082), 0.377 (standard error = 0.023, critical ratio = 16.391), and 0.822 (standard error = 0.076, critical ratio = 10.816) respectively. They are all statistically significant at the 0.05 level. Next, the three newly added regression paths are analyzed. QP ← CV (H5) is −0.088 (standard error = 0.222) and non-significant (critical ratio = −0.396). Thus, CV does not directly affect QP. QM ← CV (H6) is −0.087 (standard error = 0.094) and also non-significant (critical ratio = −0.926). Finally, QR ← CV (H7) is 0.082 (standard error = 0.104) and is also non-significant at the 0.05 level (critical ratio = 0.789). Thus, CV does not directly affect QM or QR.

Given that H5, H6, and H7 are all not accepted, the alternative model is indeed incorrect. Therefore, the hypothesis that quality climate, as an important intermediary in bridging cultural values into quality practices

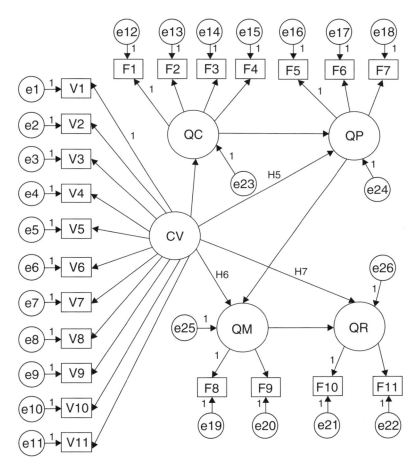

Figure 6.5 Alternative model of Chinese cultural values of TQM.

and results, is supported. The standardized output of the alternative model is shown in Figure 6.6. Meanwhile, this section on SEM concludes with the full model as a feasible model explaining the inter-relationships among Chinese cultural values and quality management.

Conclusion on quantitative findings

The quantitative analyses performed in the present study have concluded with two important points. Firstly, the study has suggested a comprehensive framework of quality management through exploring the DoD's (1992) TQM model and has supported its veracity

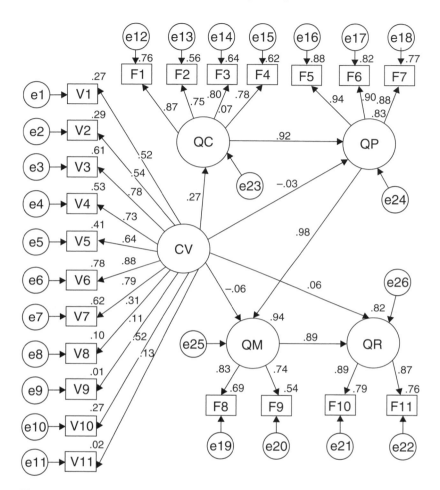

Figure 6.6 Standardized output of alternative model.

through testing it with actual data gathered from the industry. This four-variable framework incorporating quality climate, processes, methods, and results follows a process model of quality management (Shuster, 1990). The model also points to the importance of management nurturing a total quality climate (Bounds *et al.*, 1994). The process model and quality climate are important theories underlying this framework as discussed in Chapter 2. Secondly, the study has extended Anderson *et al.*'s (1994) ARS theory and developed a theoretical model on the impact of national culture on TQM. This model, in the case of Chinese cultural values, has been empirically tested using actual data. The evidence on the significant impact of national culture on quality climate supports the central argument of the theory of the culture-specific TQM.

However, what is left undone at this stage is to find out in more detail the characteristics of the Chinese-style TQM as argued to exist. The quantitative analyses performed could only support that there is indeed a relationship between TQM and Chinese cultural values or that a theoretical model of cultural influence on TQM can be developed. As to how Chinese cultural values are manifested in TQM activities, quantitative analyses can hardly tell much. In order to explore further, qualitative analyses have to be conducted. In-depth interviews conducted with three ISO 9000 companies operating in Hong Kong and mainland China are presented in Chapter 7. It is hoped that through qualitative inquiries, the characteristics of a Chinese-style TQM model could be explored and related back to the quantitative findings obtained in this chapter.

7
Case Studies

In this chapter, three case studies of ISO 9000 certified companies operating in mainland China and Hong Kong are presented. Through their success stories, some salient features of how they manage quality in the Chinese way are highlighted. Relating these characteristics back to the theoretical elements as empirically tested in the culture-specific TQM model, a schematic framework describing the influence of Chinese cultural values on TQM activities is proposed.

An interpretive approach to TQM

Traditional research paradigms can roughly be divided into two namely, positivism and interpretivism. Allan (1998) pointed out that research on quality management is not located in any of these two paradigms. She proudly labeled quality management research as 'shamelessly eclectic' because it is believed that no one single paradigm is sufficient to capture all the parameters of the research questions (p. S4). Therefore, the two research approaches can be used alternatively, together, or even interchangeably as deemed appropriate. Case study research as an interpretive and qualitative method has a long tradition in the social sciences and is important to the building of organizational and management theories (see for example, Eisenhardt, 1989, 1991; Dyer and Wilkins, 1991). More uses of this approach have already been called for by the TQM research community (Simon *et al.*, 1994; Sohal *et al.*, 1994). Recently, Leonard and McAdam (2000) also advocated the use of more advanced qualitative methods such as grounded theory methodology (Glaser and Strauss, 1967) in TQM research.

In Chapter 6, the impact of Chinese cultural values on TQM has been evaluated on statistical grounds. However, statistical results can often only demonstrate the existence of relationships. In order to understand in more depth how these Chinese cultural values are actually influencing TQM in practice, real life examples have to be drawn upon through interviews and case studies. Simon *et al.* (1994) reckoned that the generative case study research method involves three phases. Firstly, crucial concepts are generated using different methods such as literature review, observations, interviews, and document content analysis. Then, the themes of the research are elaborated through open-ended, non-standardized interviews so as to 'flesh out' the underlying concepts. Finally, the 'fleshed out' concepts are formally measured and tested so as to achieve triangulation (Denzin, 1989). Similarly, the present study follows a more traditional type of triangulation where data obtained from the generative case studies are to enrich and interpret the quantitative finding which in turn is based on sound theory and literature review. This chapter provides three case studies of three Chinese companies operating in Hong Kong and mainland China. As cultural values are deeply embedded in the members of the organizations, it is through knowing their behaviors and day to day activities, analyzing their personal and corporate mottoes, and learning from some critical incidences that such underlying values be inferred to.

Since the present study has devoted a substantial portion of its resources to generate a theoretical model based on empirical data, the three case studies serve here as a secondary source mainly to validate and to enrich the quantitative finding. As such, the case study research is conducted in a more casual and free-form style, aiming to generate descriptive accounts of the companies' success stories. More formal procedures towards the case study methodology can be referred to in the well-documented works of, for example, Yin (1989) and Eisenhardt (1989, 1991). All interviews were conducted in January 1999 with the senior director or manager responsible for the implementation of quality management activities. When available, the human resource director joined in for discussion. The meetings usually started with a thorough plant visit, followed by in-depth interviews at the plant office. Corporate publications such as yearbook, brochures, and the like were provided. No tape recording was used as the interviewees expressed feelings of uneasiness with the presence of a tape recorder. A list of interview questions, written in Chinese, was given to the interviewees well in advance. The questions mainly focused on three areas. The first area covers background data such as company history, size, production output, achievements, and short- or long-term plans. The second area covers mainly the interviewees' attitude towards Chinese cultural values and their relevance to managing quality. Here, information as to the four dimensions of TQM namely: (1) quality climate; (2) processes; (3) methods; and (4) results were also gathered. The last area concerns with the salient characteristics of a Chinese TQM company. Although semi-structured interview questions were used, most of the time the interviewees were encouraged to provide critical incidences or interesting stories rather than to adhere strictly to the question formats. All interviews were conducted in Cantonese or Putonghua. The interviews often continued in a more relaxed manner over a cup of tea after formal interviews of about two hours. With the exception of the first case study where partial anonymity was requested by the interviewee, all names and figures are factual. The US dollar amounts are approximate due to conversion from the original currencies. For the two interviews conducted in mainland China, two other researchers accompanied the author and took simple notes together. After the interviews, the notes were compared and discussed.

The three cases are firstly presented descriptively in the following sections. An attempt is then made to 'flesh out' the important concepts underlying them and to relate them back to the quantitative finding. In particular, the dimensional elements of the culture-specific TQM model are elaborated. The final objective is to highlight some important characteristics of the Chinese-style TQM.

Case 1: SW Electric

SW Electric (SWE) is a designer and manufacturer of high quality electric components for automobiles, plant machinery, and household appliances. Founded in 1959 by the late Shanghainese Mr SW and his wife, SWE was the first manufacturing operation of its kind in Hong Kong.

SW Electric started as a manufacturer of toy components. As the Hong Kong toy industry experienced rapid growth in the 1960s, SWE was able to attain high sales volume and achieve economies of scale. It soon started to diversify into producing automobile and industrial components. With Mr RW, son of the late chairman joining in 1972, SWE penetrated also the home appliance component market with high quality products. Mr RW took over as chief executive in 1996 and turned SWE into a major supplier of component parts to leading multi-nationals in the United States and Europe. With manufacturing plants in Southern China and Thailand; R&D headquarters in Germany, Switzerland, and the United States; sales and marketing offices in the United States, Japan, and Hong Kong, SW Electric is today the second largest manufacturer of its kind in the world; 1998 was a record year for SW Electric in spite of the Asian economic turmoil. Consolidated profit after tax increased to around US$81 million, a dramatic raise of 43 per cent as compared to that of 1997. From the perspective of the shareholders, SWE represents an ideal investment as earnings per share and dividend per share rose 43 per cent and 30 per cent respectively.

SW Electric employs all the major tools and techniques to maintain its high product quality. Zero defect, statistical process control throughout all manufacturing processes, failure mode and effects analysis, quality function deployment, and just-in-time inventory methods are all effectively adopted. SWE's plant in Southern China was certified by ISO 9000 in 1994 and has today attained the highest quality standard in the industry, allowing it to produce parts for the American automobile giants such as Ford and General Motors. Monthly production in China is expected to soon reach 16 million units to cope with the continual growth of the company and the anticipated expanding demand. In 1998, Mr RW was elected Asian businessman of the year by a major business periodical publisher.

Quality climate in SWE

The corporate mission of SWE is to achieve a harmonious and ever improving life for people as its corporate slogan says 'Making your life better'. Management at SWE believes that this can be achieved by emphasizing learning and education as well as commitment to society. The management philosophy of SWE, as brought down from the late Mr SW, is based on a traditional Chinese saying literally meaning 'The kind of wood you get depends on which hill you go to'. This reflects a Chinese emphasis on situation orientation and adaptiveness through active pursuit of a desirable life. Mr RW strongly believes that a Chinese company should be vigilant throughout the surrounding environment and constantly absorb new knowledge. No matter Western or Eastern, as long as what is good for the long-term well being of the organization, people should learn and adopt.

Mr RW himself is an excellent example of a learning man constantly searching for good management methods and disseminating them to his subordinates. For example, he picks up many ideas from an annual seminar held at the Harvard Business School and then adapts them to his own philosophy. Very often he would distribute books on management, which he finds useful to the members of his management team. This is often followed by personal or group discussions of the topics in the books. It is through Mr RW's constant desire and commitment to learn new things that SWE's solid foundation on quality has become its cutting edge.

Mr DP, senior manager for quality management, recalled how Mr RW started the quality education in SWE through grasping the essence of the Chinese people's psychology. One vivid example is the story of 'bathroom culture'. In the early 1980s, when SWE's China plant first went into operation, Mr RW realized that to attain high quality production, he must firstly educate the mainland Chinese workers. He also realized that education and change need time and any coercive actions will only result in failure. Therefore, he decided to begin by changing the often ignored daily behaviors of the workers. Since most of the workers in the China plant were relatively less educated and many of them came from remote villages, the bathrooms in the plant were often unimaginably dirty and hygiene condition was nearly hopeless. Mr RW decided to launch a 'bathroom complaint campaign' and personally encouraged workers to file complaints whenever they find the bathrooms in bad condition. The campaign soon reached a peak and the workers began to realize that complaints do not help. They started to become more self-disciplined and the cleanliness of the bathrooms improved. Mr RW, knowing that the underlying value of the Chinese people is based on harmony, took this opportunity to instill into the minds of the workers the quality principles, explaining personally to them the importance of cleanliness in the bathrooms, the workplace, the canteen, and even at the workers' homes. When the condition of the workplace has reached a certain standard, Mr RW further used the example of the 'bathroom complaint' incident to educate the workers the importance of quality, drawing metaphors to explain to the workers the feeling of a dissatisfied customer.

Mr RW strongly believes in the Chinese saying that things have to improve gradually while an abrupt increase in anything deems to be a failure. This is even reflected in the Chinese name of SWE, which literally means 'inch by inch'. From a manufacturing plant with the dirtiest bathrooms in Southern China to one which produces the highest quality electric components in the world; from workers with relatively low education to workers who can truly grasp the basic principles of quality, SWE has achieved these through gradual education and improvement.

Quality processes in SWE

The underlying purpose of SWE getting the ISO 9000 certification is to improve its product quality through strengthening its quality management system. The process of getting the certification also reflects some elements of Chinese culture, especially the value of familism.

As the successor of a family-run business, Mr RW strives to make SWE a big family of 15 000 men. Instead of hiring a quality consultant to install the ISO 9000 system like in many Western companies, SWE installed the system entirely by itself. Mr RW believes that hiring an outside consultant will only bring many abrupt changes which may distort the harmony of the big family. Therefore, he started by sending employees to training courses on quality and ISO 9000. The trained employees, often managers and front line supervisors, would then teach their own subordinates their learnt knowledge. The certification journey of SWE was thus much longer but Mr RW believes that results have been much more fruitful. With the first certification of a four-phase program in 1994, SWE had already embarked on a formal TQM program.

Mr RW understands that to maintain high quality, people have to constantly learn new knowledge. SW Electric has a vigorous training scheme for each and every employee. The training needs of each staff are identified and appropriate training given without delay. Results of training and identification of new training needs are periodically reviewed. Furthermore, employees are highly encouraged to identify and request the type of training they feel lacking. Whenever, there is a job vacancy, internal staffs who have received the appropriate training or possess multi-talent are firstly considered. The idea is to make each and every employee feel like a member of the caring family and that his or her well being is considered as the foremost priority.

Staff evaluation in SWE is based on performance but not in the conventional Western 'management by objective' way. Budgets are set with top management, middle management, and front-line management taking budget horizons of five years, two years, and one year respectively. The attitude towards the budget in SWE is flexible. Furthermore, budgets are not tools for penalizing low achievers but instead are opportunities for problem identification and problem solving. Mr RW believes that SWE takes the best from both Western and Chinese management styles. The former emphasizes on building up a system to be followed by all employees while the latter underscores the maintenance of harmonious human relations. He believes that when human relations are harmonious, people will respect the system and thus take every necessary step to adhere to it.

Mr DP recalled an incident when a worker accidentally damaged a very expensive mold during production. The worker ran home immediately fearing of punishment. Mr RW on knowing the accident, sent the front-line supervisor to the worker's home and invited him back to the plant. There was no punishment of any kind but Mr RW, together with the supervisor, taught the worker the proper handling of the mold and let him work on the task again. It is Mr RW's belief in the Chinese saying 'We are all on the same boat' that a harmonious human relation leads the employees to adhere to the organizational system, no matter it is a performance budget at the management level or a standard work procedure in the workshop.

It is also due to this harmonious human relation that firing in SWE is rare. In an interview given by Mr RW when he was elected Asian businessman of the year, he promised his people that no one would be fired in spite of the recent recession. Mr DP further added that firing is not the personnel policy at SWE. During periods of low production, the 'redundant' employees are given training or retraining to meet more demanding standards when the situation improves. At the same time, hiring of new employees is frozen. Only when situation demands, annual raises are stopped for low performers. Mr DP commented that the management style in SWE is a hybrid of Chinese and Western styles but the tendency is more towards the Chinese emphasis on collectivism and trust rather than the result orientation in traditional Western management. He claimed that a Chinese company which one can be proud of is able to learn from the West the establishment of a clear and well-structured organizational system and to use this system to reinforce trust among employees.

Quality methods in SWE

In terms of the hard aspects, SWE has a strong commitment to research and development backed up by its international team of experienced engineers and designers. With the use of computer aided design, SWE is able to progressively push forward the frontiers with highly innovative products and manufacturing methods holding international patents.

Each production facility in SWE has its own training center within which both management and workers alike are taught the latest in manufacturing and quality control. Statistical process control techniques are practiced throughout all manufacturing processes and all workers are trained to meet zero defect at all production stages. Engineers, laboratory analysts, and designers use modern methods such as Taguchi methods, orthogonal experiments, failure mode effect analysis, and quality function deployment to ensure the highest product quality. SW Electric also employs a vertically integrated manufacturing process so that it is possible to maintain high standards for production parts as the tooling and fixtures are made in-house. This feature allows a customer's request to be custom-made, turning out a prototype exceptionally fast, and transferring new parts into production at high volumes.

In terms of the soft aspect or human aspect, Mr DP stated that SWE has always been emphasizing on collectivism. Therefore, group activities such as QCC have been active since the late 1970s. The QCCs in SWE are all voluntary. To encourage active participation in the circles, annual circle report presentations and contests are held. When SWE first held its QCC contest, an impressive number of 880 workers participated. Management and workers alike were unexpectedly enthusiastic about the event but they deemed it a failure. What happened was that only one winning circle was selected and as a result the members of the other circles demonstrated low morale. This valuable experience has reminded the management of SWE the real meaning of Chinese collectivism and that transferring the QCC activity as it is successful in Japan to Chinese soil is not possible. The winning criterion was thus changed. Whenever a circle's report is evaluated a mark of 80 or above, the circle is a winner. This evaluation criterion was quickly accepted by the circles and up until today, QCC activities are highly active.

Apart from QCC activities, individual suggestions are also welcomed. However, SWE does not emphasize too much on individual talent since it adheres to its ultimate corporate philosophy of being a big but harmonious family. Therefore, winning circles are awarded a trophy, cash bonus, and are taken photos with the chief executive. On the other hand, if it is an individual suggestion, the winner is awarded a trophy only. Mr DP claimed that most Chinese workers, especially those in the mainland China plant, welcome the trophy and the photo rather than the cash. This is due to the cultural characteristic of 'face' of the Chinese people. Showing the photo taken with the chief executive to family members, relatives, and friends represents a kind of honor which cannot be bought at any price.

The message of quality at SWE is well understood by all levels of employees. Every employee is requested to carry a small card in which the 'SW Spirit' and the 'SW Quality Statement' is written. Employees are requested to read the statement every morning. To create a harmonious and familial atmosphere, employees frequently hold activities in the plant canteen during lunchtime. An example is a simple contest in which employees are asked to recite the 'SW Spirit' and the 'SW Quality Statement' quickly and accurately. Winners are awarded a free soda and so on. Of course, the spirit is not on getting a free soda but to create an environment where collectivism is valued.

Quality results in SWE

According to Mr DP, the certification of ISO 9000 has helped SWE to improve its quality management system greatly. For example, through fulfilling the ISO 9000 requirements, there are now complete and systematic operating procedures concerning all aspects from design and pre-production to selling and distribution. This helps to minimize errors through standardizing the operating procedures. Also, SWE's effort in embarking on a TQM journey has obviously been harvesting. For example, aiming at zero defect, the defective rate in each production step has now been minimized to less than one per cent. Results from the '*gemba kaizen*' campaign have also been satisfactory.

Nevertheless, Mr DP remarked that the most valuable improvement is in terms of customer relations. He stressed that high quality products can of course delight customers but SWE has a completely different view on customer relation from that as seen in most Western companies. Mr RW constantly emphasizes that not only members inside SWE are riding on the same boat and should thus maintain good harmony. In fact, SWE and its customers are also riding on the same boat. That is to say, the well being of SWE depends also on the well being of its customers. For a company which is in real harmony, interdependence should extend out of its organizational boundaries. Mr DP cited one good example of this extended interdependence. A producer of a rather old-fashioned hair dryer once sought for an order of an odd type component whose production has been stopped some time ago. Instead of rejecting this odd order as many companies might naturally do, Mr RW and his designers requested for a meeting with this producer. In the meeting, they explained to the producer how both parties could benefit if the product design would change slightly to accommodate another type of component. The two parties worked together to find out the best solution, ending up with a delighted customer and a successful order for SWE. Mr DP believes that Chinese people live on mutual harmony and reciprocity. The mutual support between the two parties has led to a continuous business relationship until today and is expected to continue in the future.

Case 2: Jinling group company limited

Jinling Group Company Limited is a consortium of 11 manufacturing companies situated in Jiangmen city of the Guangdong province in mainland China. Jinling manufactures high quality home appliances with a specialization in washing machines and air-conditioners. In 1994, the washing machine plant and the air-conditioner plant entered into joint venture agreements with the Hong Kong Wo Kee Hong (Group) Company Limited and the Mitsubishi Heavy Industries in Japan respectively. These agreements gave birth to the two core companies of the group namely, the Jinling Electrical Company Limited and the Mitsubishi Heavy Industries-Jinling Air-Conditioners Company Limited.

The group first started its operations in 1983 with around US$170 000 worth of production. In a relatively short period of 12 years' time, Jinling was able to increase its production value by 1000 per cent. Today, Jinling boasts an annual production of 300 000 home air-conditioners, 500 000 washing machines, and 2 600 000 electric fans. The products of this 3600-employee group are sold nationally to all major provinces in China and are also exported to other South-east Asian and Middle-east countries.

The group was certified under ISO 9000 in 1996 and is included in the 500 largest industrial enterprises in China. Since 1986, Jinling's washing machines have been attaining the highest production and exportation volume in the country. Using the latest production technology from Germany and Italy, Jinling received numerous national awards from the various State Commissions. In 1997, Jinling's washing machine production was further awarded the American Underwriters' Laboratories (UL) certification, making Jinling the first and only manufacturer in China to possess such an internationally recognized quality.

Quality climate in Jinling

The Jinling Washing Machine Factory, which has now grown to become the Jiangmen Jinling Group, was founded by Mr Wu Qunxing in 1983. The guiding philosophy of Mr Wu is based on a Chinese saying which can be literally translated as 'He who desires to establish, let others establish also; He who desires to achieve, let others achieve also'. It is based on this philosophy that Jinling has nurtured a profound corporate vision to contribute to the growth of China's state enterprises through continuous self-improvement. To achieve this long-term vision, Jinling has successfully built up an enterprise spirit based on three elements namely, consciousness, independence, and coordination. 'Consciousness' refers to the desire for self-initiated learning, self-initiated labor, and self-initiated cultivation. 'Independence' refers to the ability to work independently and the ability to demonstrate personal qualities. 'Coordination' refers to collectivism, cooperation, patience, and forgiveness. Mr Wu urges for total commitment towards such qualities in work, learning, and other daily endeavors.

In order to realize Mr Wu's motto to life and to bring the people of Jinling closer to the ideal 'Jinling Men', Mr Wu calls for total participation in quality improvement. He takes a more traditional Chinese approach by acting as a father figure to initiate a total quality movement and to lead everyone in the group towards this objective. In 1996, he initiated a company-wide quality policy education. Understanding that people at different levels of the organization have different duties and skills, he requested all middle level managers to take written examinations on quality management principles and all production line supervisors to undergo training. The examinations helped Jinling to further solidify the foundation of its quality after obtaining the ISO 9000 certification.

According to Mr Liao, senior quality manager of Jinling who has returned to China in the early 1980s after substantial TQC training in Japan, the management style that Mr Wu adheres to is a mixture of paternalistic and participative management. Under this management style, which he claimed as following the socialist 'democratic centralism', all employees at all levels are requested to provide suggestions and ideas which are thoroughly discussed and understood. After this, each department or unit will furnish departmental reports to be submitted to top management, which essentially is composed of Mr Wu and a few top leaders, for final decision-making. Although this so-called management style does not appear to be distinctive from the familiar bottom-up approach, Mr Liao reckoned that it is a successful style which incorporates traditional Chinese paternalistic management and what people call 'industrial democracy' after the political reform of China. As pointed out by Mr Liao, the Chinese people have always been group oriented and collective decision-making has been a method to preserve group harmony. However, due to the rise of communism, many of the positive aspects of traditional Confucianism were actually buried by the rising power. Since then, Chinese management had become one which was totally based on centralization and authoritarianism. As the political situation has changed during the past ten years, Chinese managers were allowed to revisit the positive aspects of Confucianism and at the same time absorb good management styles and techniques from foreign sources. It is a result of this gradual change that Jinling has adopted a management style which incorporates both the traditional Chinese value of paternalism and a modernized view on democracy. He also mentioned that the present political situation in China does have a profound impact on all state owned enterprises. Its gradual change has also been leading the change in management styles of these enterprises. It can be said that the organizational climate of state owned enterprises in China is actually a microscopic view of the country's overall political climate.

With the reform and open door policy of China in gradual progress, the underlying traditional values of the Chinese people, so deeply embedded but were once oppressed, are gradually re-emerging. What is important is not to commit the same mistake which communism has committed by throwing away all the traditional values of the people even when they are of good nature. Jinling, like the country herself, is gradually revisiting and re-emphasizing the positive aspects of traditional values. For example, paternalism in the past had been abused and had become a tool for people to centralize their powers. In fact, the correct interpretation of the Confucian teaching of paternalism is on the creation of a successful and respectable leadership through propriety and benevolence. Many of the Confucian teachings are in fact in line with the characteristics of good management. It is only that people in the past have misinterpreted them.

Quality processes in Jinling

According to Mr Liao, Jinling provides a three-month training program to all new entrants. The program consists of four main areas namely: (1) company history and development; (2) corporate culture; (3) technical skills; and (4) safety. In order to let all employees grasp a clearer view of the operations, even university graduates who may be taking up posts outside the assembly lines are put to receive six months' training on the various manufacturing processes. Training on quality management techniques is also given to all production workers. However, workers at different levels are provided with different degrees of quality knowledge. For example, line supervisors are trained to use the various control charts and to interpret collected data, while front-line workers are trained only to collect production data. Nevertheless, they are all taught the fundamental concepts of ISO 9000 and TQM during specially arranged meetings.

In line with Mr Wu's practice, examinations are given to employees after each training session. These examinations represent also the main criteria for performance evaluation. Under normal market conditions, a staff on failing an examination three times will usually be laid off. Mr Liao stated that most employees welcome this examination system because it is objective and helps to transmit a clear message to employees on what kind of performance is expected from them. He further added that the creation of a competitive working environment is in line with Deng Xiaopeng's philosophy on pragmatism. Due to this competitive working environment, employee turnover in Jinling is very low.

Quality methods in Jinling

In order to disseminate and to better coordinate total quality activities, Jinling has installed a TQC office. The TQC office has recently adopted another quality control technique known as 'management QC point' (*kanri ten*). In fact, Jinling is able to absorb and implement effectively various Japanese production and TQM techniques. For example, the TQC office is responsible for organizing QCC activities. Each production department has now about three to five QCCs. Basically, Jinling's QCCs are quite different from the ones seen in Japanese companies. Apart from that they all use the same tools such as statistical control charts, pareto charts, and fishbone diagrams, Jinling's QCCs did not start as voluntary circles like in Japan. The TQC office understands that due to a difference in the standard of living in China and Japan, it is not impossible but difficult to expect voluntary participation in QCC activities. The TQC office thus first started by assigning some task groups with the intention to tackle some specific problems. The task groups were taught the seven tools and the basic operations of QCCs. Results of successful problem solving were posted on bulletin boards inside the factory and task group members were awarded cash bonus. At the same time, the TQC office encouraged each production department to form their own QCCs. Today, Jinling organizes QCC case report presentations every year. Winning circles are awarded cash benefits. Through the efforts by the QCCs and the now implemented campaign of 'one suggestion per person', Jinling is able to reduce its average defective rate of each production department to about two per cent. With the use of the *kanri ten* system, Jinling is now heading towards the goal of zero defect. Furthermore, to emphasize the importance of internal customer satisfaction, there are monthly cross production process meetings when workers of different assembly lines or processes meet and exchange experiences and suggestions.

Quality results in Jinling

According to Mr Liao, the certification under ISO 9000 has brought substantial benefits. It has assisted Jinling to set up a strong foundation for its quality management system so that product quality could be further strengthened. As a result, Jinling has become the first washing machine manufacturer in China to obtain the UL certification. Most important of all, the certification has helped to create a strong quality consciousness among its workers.

Concerning the area of customer orientation, Mr Liao stated that Jinling's attitude to customers has always been following the Chinese saying of 'Do not to others what you do not want others do to you'. He attributed three different elements to the three types of customers of Jinling. The relationship with wholesalers is based on trust because what they face is usually not a problem with product quality but their own liquidity problem. Without trust and understanding of the wholesalers' financial difficulties, it is not possible to establish long-term trading relationships. The relationship with retailers is based on sincerity. Jinling understands that to encourage retailers to sell Jinling's products, Jinling must demonstrate the willingness to cooperate and support them. Thus, Jinling places particular emphasis on after-sales services by establishing 18 after-sales counters covering as far away as Urumqi in Xinjiang province to support the retailers. Finally, the relationship with consumers is simply based on quality. In Jinling, every member adheres to 'customer is the king'.

Case 3: Dachangjiang group company limited

Founded in 1992, the Dachangjiang Group is a large-scale Sino-foreign joint venture enterprise situated in Jiangmen city of the Guangdong province in China. Specializing in manufacturing motorcycles and engine parts, the 1900 employee Dachangjiang Group is composed of two core manufacturing plants namely, G.L. River Motorcycle Manufacturing Company Limited and Hualing Precision Machinery Company Limited. The former is one of the largest motorcycle manufacturer in China possessing 27 production lines arranged in a multi-purpose factory which covers an area of 55 000 square meters. The latter is one of the most modern engine manufacturers in Asia equipped with 23 production lines covering an area of 44 500 square meters. The group includes in all major provinces of China, a sales network of 26 sales branches and 2500 exclusive sales departments and authorized distributors, and a service network of 20 service centers and 2000 contracted maintenance shops.

The US$170 million invested group boasts an annual production output of 800 000 motorcycles and engines. Dachangjiang currently produces nine models of motorcycles under the Haojue series. All products are produced using technologies imported from Suzuki Motor Corporation in Japan and are evaluated by the China National Motorcycle Testing Center and Suzuki itself as having the same high quality standard as the 'made in Japan' models.

The Dachangjiang Group has been practicing TQM since 1995 and was certified under ISO 9000 in 1997 by the Guangdong Audit and

Certification Center of Quality Systems in China and TUV Rheinland in Germany. The corporate objective of the group is to increase its annual motorcycle production level to 1 000 000 units by the year 2005. Although, Dachangjiang does rely on imported Japanese technologies, it also takes a domestic initiative towards research and development by cooperating with science institutes and manufacturing companies in Japan and Europe. Dachangjiang has its own technology development center, its own market research department, and its own team of professional experts, integrating the entire series of production processes, from modeling to designing, to manufacturing, and to testing. In order to satisfy the market, Dachangjiang has achieved world class ability to develop its own motorcycle engines, bodies, electrical parts, and outlook designs.

Quality climate in Dachangjiang

The corporate motto of Dachangjiang, which can be seen written all over the plant site, is a Chinese saying which literally means 'everything depends on your effort'. It is this positive attitude towards life that has made Dachangjiang one of the most successful joint venture endeavors in Southern China. Mr Zhou, senior manager of the quality management department of G.L. River, described the group's management philosophy as putting foremost emphasis on its employees. As the corporate slogan states 'To provide top quality products to users through unremitting effort; to create better future for society through hard work', Mr Zhou said that everything starts with the employees. He believed that through constantly improving employees' well being, employee satisfaction would lead to customer satisfaction.

Understanding that management by objective frequently contradicts with employee benefit, Dachangjiang's strategy is to use employee benefit to achieve management objectives. Mr Zhou cited some examples of management objectives. At present, the mid-term objectives are of four main areas and are all quantified. In terms of product quality, Dachangjiang strives to achieve 100 per cent Suzuki quality. In terms of national industry recognition, Dachangjiang aims to be the first in class. In terms of sales/production ratio, Dachangjiang aims to increase from the now 96 per cent to 100 per cent. As to customer satisfaction, Dachangjiang aims at 100 per cent total satisfaction. To achieve these, it is only through the effort of its employees, and the best way to induce full effort is by fulfilling their needs. Mr Pei, manager of the human resource department, mentioned that Dachangjiang offers the best wages of all manufacturing companies in Jiangmen city. It also offers the best employee benefit scheme which includes a free flat to all employees upon their marriage. To upgrade the human quality of its workers, Dachangjiang places particular emphasis on training and QCC activities whereby monetary as well as intangible awards are given. As a whole, Dachangjinag believes in first creating satisfied employees, then satisfied customers.

Mr Zhou reckoned that after the reform of China from a planned economy to a market economy, interference from the central government has largely reduced. Many Chinese companies are now able and are proud to compete with their Western counterparts through continuous quality improvement. He believed that the best Chinese management style is one that is able to assimilate foreign technologies in order to unleash the maximum capability of the Chinese people. The Chinese people are potentially industrious. However, this property was unable to be fully appreciated before the reform of China due to restrictions in absorbing foreign technologies. Today, Dachangjiang is able to fully utilize the hard working quality of the Chinese people through fusion with the latest foreign technologies, including the Japanese way of TQM and the Western quality standards of ISO 9000. In particular, he attributed Dachangjiang's success in quality to three underlying values of the Chinese people namely, the values of collectivism, situation orientation, and adaptiveness. Dachangjiang has, since its inception in 1992, continuously and gradually expended efforts in new product development. Management at Dachangjiang understands that success is a matter of gradual accumulation of experience and knowledge but not an abrupt change. This clearly reflects the Chinese value of situation orientation. It is also due to the adaptiveness of the Chinese people that Dachangjiang has successfully absorbed Suzuki technologies in its production and is proud that not one Japanese engineer has ever come to station in Dachangjiang to supervise its productions. The relationship that Dachangjiang has with Suzuki is one that is built on mutual cooperation but not dominance.

Quality processes in Dachangjiang

Dachangjiang has basically adopted the ISO 9000 standards as the blueprint for its quality management system. This helps to enhance continuous consistency in the production of quality products. Mr Zhou realized that the present quality management system is still insufficient and has since 1995, gradually implemented a company-wide TQM process. At the same time, employee benefits are also upgraded in order to encourage total participation.

After the successful implementation of the 5S campaign, Dachangjiang's TQM activities are now in full vigor since 1999. Some obvious results can be seen from the 5S campaign. For example, the previous 22 per cent defective rate of the painting line has now reduced to 92 per cent 'right at the first time' and is expected to catch up with the Suzuki rate of 96 per cent. As TQM is a continuous endeavor involving all employees and external suppliers, obvious results are still to be anticipated.

Mr Pei mentioned that the implementation of TQM in Dachangjiang requires close cooperation between the quality management department and the human resource department. A typical training program for a new entrant includes a training seminar on corporate culture, in which employees are briefed the basic management philosophy and some historical development of Dachangjiang and the code of conduct for being a corporate citizen. Basic quality control, work process, and safety training are also given during a one-week period. What is of particular importance as Mr Pei said is that the purpose of training is to instill a sense of self-improvement in the employees. He added that due to the reform of China, people can no longer adhere to the mentality of relying on the iron rice bowl as in the past. People in Dachangjiang are taught the importance of self-improvement and the spirit of 'we are all on the same boat'. Mr Zhou also believed that the Chinese people are basically collective in nature and mutual improvement of the self and the organization is by constant education.

Quality methods in Dachangjiang

What is so special about Dachangjiang is that its adaptiveness and situation orientation allows it to learn and absorb foreign technologies and to come up with a system which completely belongs to itself. Understanding that its Haojue series of motorcycles is targeted for the domestic market, what Dachangjiang needs from Suzuki in Japan is its basic production technology only but not an entire replication of Suzuki and its products in China. Dachangjiang is able to use Japanese technologies to produce products of the same internationally recognized quality to cater for the needs of the domestic market, thus creating a Chinese product that Chinese people can be proud of. This attitude towards learning and refinement is also seen in Dachangjiang's quality control methods. For example, Dachangjiang is proud to utilize statistical process control and diagnosis (SPCD) which is an advanced type of statistical process control method developed by a Chinese Professor known as Zhang Gongxu at the Beijing University of Science and Technology. Statistical process control and diagnosis is an example of the Chinese people's ability to draw lessons from the experiences of Japan and the United States. It has made a major breakthrough to be the world's first multivariate statistical diagnosis theory since Walter Shewhart's quality control theory. In fact, Professor Zhang is now researching on another advanced stage of SPCD known as SPCDA (statistical process control, diagnosis, and adjustment) (Zhang, 1999).

In terms of group activities, Dachangjiang started to introduce QCCs in 1995. After three years of gradual expansion, the QCC activities have grown to a company-wide implementation in 1998. The foremost objective of introducing QCC activities in Dachangjiang is to upgrade human quality through enhancement of creativity and experience exchange. Although problem solving is only the second reason for implementing QCCs, the problem-solving rate of the 69 QCCs at present is about 89 per cent.

To enhance the growth of QCCs, management at Dachangjiang takes a gradual approach by arranging three types of QCCs. The first type resembles task forces which are compulsory for all employees to participate upon the need to firefight critical problems. The second type is known as instructive QCCs with improvement topics provided by management. The third type is completely voluntary and self-initiated. Mr Zhou remarked that QCCs are a good way to enhance employee motivation because monetary bonus and other awards are given to circle members when good suggestions are given. The annual QCC presentation also represents a kind of honor which employees accept with good response. Apart from QCCs, Dachangjiang also encourages individual suggestions in the form of 'one suggestion per worker per month'. As seen on the bulletin boards inside the factory plant, the monthly individual suggestion participation rate frequently reaches over 90 per cent of the number of employees. Mr Pei said that each worker would get a small amount of cash bonus for each suggestion given. The emphasis is to keep the workers think constantly and to be creative.

Dachangjiang also extends its QCC activities beyond itself to suppliers. At present, 12 inter-company QCCs are formed with the 200 suppliers of Dachangjiang. The purpose is to create a harmonious relationship with them so that Dachangjiang can understand their situations and needs and to better coordinate and cooperate. Dachangjiang also takes the initiative to encourage suppliers to attain ISO 9000 certification by providing technical support and most encouraging of all, a cash bonus of up to US$1200 for successful certification. In order to produce products of the highest quality, Dachangjiang knows how to take a lead role in cooperating with suppliers through sincerity, trust, and harmony.

Quality results in Dachangjiang

Mr Zhou mentioned that apart from the hard facts that implementing ISO 9000 and TQM does help Dachangjiang to reduce defective rates and to increase problem solving rates and so on, the most important point is to use the concept of quality management to upgrade human quality. He pointed out that Chinese people are traditionally collective and like to keep themselves in good harmony. However, due to these underlying values, Chinese people sometimes demonstrate some negative aspects of their values. For example, in order to save face and to preserve good interpersonal harmony, Chinese people may not tell all the truth in some circumstances. This may lead people not to devote entirely towards a certain endeavor. Having a good management system can help to redirect the attitude to the right track. The idea here is not to use TQM to replace the traditional Chinese values, which is actually impossible. Rather it is to use TQM to induce the healthy aspects of these traditional values. Therefore, under the system of ISO 9000 and TQM, the Chinese people are able to fully demonstrate their positive aspects and to gradually wipe out the negative side of the coin.

In terms of customer satisfaction, Dachangjiang is aiming at a 100 per cent customer satisfaction through the use of its vast network of service centers and contracted maintenance shops. The implementation of a good quality management system has enabled Dachangjiang to produce products of imported quality at homemade prices. Mr Zhou stressed that Dachangjiang's attitude towards customers is that they are the God. This is thoroughly professed among every member of Dachangjiang and is believed to be the only way for long-term corporate survival.

Findings from cases: a Chinese-style TQM

It is noticed that the three cases illustrate certain similarities as well as differences. The differences observed are mainly at the more superficial level between the operations of the Hong Kong and the mainland Chinese companies probably due to different socio-political settings. In the mainland, management techniques are more towards the mechanistic model. For example, management would put enormous emphases on quantifiable objectives. However, there has been a gradual change in the Chinese management style since the adoption of the open door policy. One good example is illustrated in the interview with Jinling. The quality manager explained that the management system there follows the socialist democratic centralism and defined it essentially as a mixture of paternalistic and participative management styles. This definition is probably very different from the Maoist understanding of democratic centralism which confronts the so-called bourgeois democracy or ultra democracy (Mao, 1972) and reflects the new socialist ideology. Putting into action in Jinling, it resembles to a certain extent the familiar management by objective system. Since Chinese state enterprises are still organized according to the structure of the Party, people would still adhere to certain communist terms such as democratic centralism.

Nevertheless, after the reform of the state owned enterprises in China, people began to realize the importance to revisit certain Confucian principles. As Lau and Kuan (1988) have commented, the real spirit of democratic centralism of socialist China was much complicated by the hegemony of the Chinese Communist Party. What is precious of the modern organizational leaders in China is their willingness to revisit and reassert the importance of traditional Confucian values and principles which were once thrown into the bonfire.

It is also found that both in the Hong Kong and mainland Chinese companies, managers have actively acknowledged the importance of Confucian values as positive towards the implementation of TQM. This similarity at the more deeply rooted philosophical level of how Chinese managers view TQM as a system influenced by Chinese cultural values is important. It is the central doctrine of the argued Chinese-style TQM. These cultural influences have to be addressed carefully and schematically related back to the quantitative findings. To this end, Table 7.1 carries some selected remarks or comments taken directly from the written transcriptions of the interviews. These sentences are then mapped back with the Chinese cultural values as obtained from the quantitative analyses.

Table 7.1   Mapping Chinese cultural values with interview statements

Harmony with nature
(S) The Chinese name of SW Electric literally means 'inch by inch'.
(J) Success is a matter of gradual accumulation of experience and knowledge, not an abrupt change.
(D) Changes need time while an abrupt change will only result in failure.

Abasement
(S) As long as what is good for the long-term well being of the company, we should learn, no matter Western or Eastern.

Table 7.1   (Continued)

(S) Mr RW picks up many ideas from the Harvard Business School and adapts them to his management philosophy.

(J) Even university graduates are put into six months' training on the assembly line.

(D) The purpose of training is to induce self-improvement.

(D) Chinese people sometimes demonstrate negative aspects of their values. But combining with a good system like TQM and ISO 9000, the negative side can be gradually corrected.

(D) Problem solving is only the second objective of QCCs. Quality control circles are to encourage experience exchange.

Situation orientation/Adaptiveness

(S) The Chinese saying 'the kind of wood you get depends on which hill you go to' has been the management philosophy of Mr SW.

(S) A Chinese company should emphasize on the surrounding environment.

(S) Quality control circles cannot be directly implemented without adjustments in Chinese soil.

(J) The best Chinese management style is able to mix the best from the West and the Chinese.

(D) Dachangjiang is proud to use Suzuki technology without even one Japanese engineer ever staying in the factory.

(D) Dachangjiang needs from Suzuki only its basic technology but not a replication of Suzuki.

(D) We use SPCD which is a Chinese invention more advanced than the Western SPC.

Respect for authority

(S) The management philosophy at SW Electric was brought down from the founder, Mr SW.

(S) Taking a photo with Mr RW is worthier than to get the trophy.

(J) Mr Wu uses a mixture of paternalistic and participative management.

(J) Employees welcome the examination system.

(J) The Confucian teaching of paternalism is to help create a respectable leader.

Interdependence/group orientation

(S) Mr RW often stresses the Chinese saying 'we are all on the same boat'.

(S) SW Electric's well being depends on its customers' well being.

(S) We would sit down together with the customer to see how to adjust the design rather than to turn down the order.

(J) The relationship with wholesalers is based on trust; with retailers, sincerity; with consumers, quality.

(D) The relationship with Suzuki is based on cooperation but not dominance.

(D) We would go all the way to Urumqi to provide assistance to our service agent.

Harmony with others

(S) Mr RW considers the well being of the employees as the first priority.

(S) Western management style emphasizes on building up a system. Chinese-style management emphasizes on maintaining human relations.

(S) When human relations are harmonious, people will respect the system.
(S) Instead of hiring an outside consultant, we send our staff to learn ISO 9000. They will then teach other staff.
(S) Having only one winning circle makes other circles' morale to drop.
(J) The Chinese have always been collective.
(J) Collective decision-making helps maintain harmony.
(J) Mr Wu stresses 'he who desires to establish, let others establish also; he who desires to achieve, let others achieve also'.
(J) Our customer focus is based on the saying 'do not to others what you do not want others do to you'.
(D) Dachangjiang's management philosophy is to put foremost emphasis on its employees.
(D) First create satisfied employees, then satisfied customers.

Other general acknowledgments on Chinese cultural values
(S) SW Electric is a hybrid of Western and Chinese management styles but the tendency is more towards the Chinese style.
(J) Confucianism is good in nature but was once neglected by communism.
(J) Chinese people are now reusing many of the Confucian principles.
(J) Confucian teachings are in line with good management.
(D) Three values are of particular importance to TQM namely, collectivism, situation orientation, and adaptiveness.

Note: S, J, and D denote remarks taken from SW Electric, Jinling, and Dachangjiang, respectively.

The attempt to map Chinese cultural values with the findings from the three cases provides substantial insight to identify important characteristics of a Chinese-style TQM. In order to systematically identify such characteristics, the relationships among the Chinese cultural values and the manifestations as provided in Table 7.1 can be further related back with the theoretical model of TQM as derived quantitatively earlier. This schematic framework can thus explicitly identify the cultural manifestations at each level of TQM implementation. As such, the main elements of a Chinese culture-specific TQM can be identified both at the underlying cultural level as well as the outer manifestation level as shown in Figure 7.1.

Chinese companies are mostly paternalistic in nature. However, the definition of paternalism as observed in those Chinese TQM companies is different. It is in a much wider sense than the ordinarily perceived meaning of concentrating power and decision-making in family hands at the top of the organization (Redding and Wong, 1986). In the Chinese-style TQM model, paternalism extends beyond the familial boundary. The leader has to play the role of not only a spiritual father figure, but also that of a member of the organization who is committed and fully participating. The leader's personal motto in life often serves

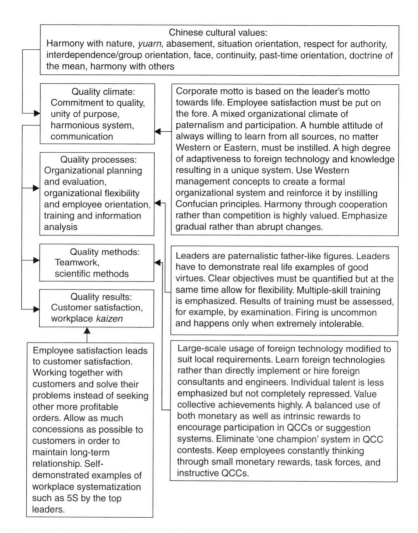

Figure 7.1   Schematic framework of Chinese-style TQM.

as the corporate motto and is instilled into the members of the organ-ization by providing them with examples. Silin (1976) noted that in the typical Chinese organization, the leader does not normally commit oneself openly to a line of action. However, as observed in the Chinese-style TQM model, the leader has to demonstrate his personal beliefs and motto by personally and very often, physically 'doing' the job.

Through giving real examples, the leader instills into the members the importance of constant learning and abasement. Thus, the hierarchical relationship as stressed in Confucianism and the participative nature of TQM have reinforced a mixed management style aiming to create a harmonious family extending beyond kinship boundaries. In fact, it has been argued that the Soviet-style one-man leadership which evolved from the founding of the People's Republic of China as well as the Party leadership style during the 1950s and 1960s are all inconsistent with the Chinese collective tradition (Smith and Wang, 1996: 323). Under a modern framework of Chinese-style management, power has been greatly decentralized. However, adhering to the golden principle of the mean, there is a clear limit for decentralization and empowerment. Organizational members are given appropriate powers to encourage participation and creativity within the custody of a benevolent and caring leader.

The high degree of adaptiveness and situation orientation has rendered the Chinese TQM companies to bravely model on available foreign technologies and knowledge. The leader has to be open-minded and has no sense of guilt to use something which is not culturally originated from Chinese soil. Rather, the motto is to learn, adapt, and render a localized version of the foreign technology. In a study of the transfer of Western marketing practices to China, Fan (1998: 205) has systematically pointed out that during the period of a centrally planned economy (1949–78), Western know-hows were regarded as capitalist evils. The attitude gradually changed during the period of 1979–92 when certain Western technical know-hows were accepted but still many were perceived as 'spiritual pollution'. Nevertheless, the situation has changed a lot from 1993 onwards when a socialist market economy was advocated. A spirit of learning from the West while guarding against any decadent influences has been seen in full force.

The value of face of the Chinese also comes into play. Although we say that the leader has to be open-minded, but if the company is able to adapt a foreign technology and to come up with an even more improved technology, this actually serves as a balance on the abasement and face-saving paradox. Just as what is seen in Dachangjiang, the managers are proud to adapt 100 per cent Suzuki technology to produce a local line of product targeted for the local market without having one Japanese engineer stationing in the production process. This high ability to adapt and the spirit of 'chasing up' is extremely important in the Chinese-style TQM model. Another good example seen in SWE is the willingness to adopt Western management techniques in order to build up a systematic organization while contextualizing it the Chinese way by reinforcing traditional Chinese values. This again illustrates a balance between the two traditional Chinese schools of thought that human is by nature good and bad.

The values of harmony with nature and harmony with people are also centrifugal to the Chinese-style TQM. The belief in gradualism as opposed to the Western emphasis on innovation and re-engineering (Hammer and Champy, 1994) is a manifestation of the value of harmony. Instead of bringing in outside consultants to induce radical changes which may distort the harmonious relationship being maintained, the Chinese TQM company would rather send employees to learn the techniques. Culturally speaking, this helps to protect the harmonious family-like atmosphere in the company from being intruded by an outsider who may bring substantial threats to the family members. Pragmatically speaking, as pointed out by SWE, this is often more cost saving also. The inter-woven values of face, abasement, familism, and harmony are so complex and delicate that any abrupt change initiated from external forces can cause serious consequences. Of course, it is not to say that Chinese TQM company does not change at all despite of changing environmental requirements. It is only that the Chinese TQM company changes by carefully observing what is in progress outside, then learns, adapts, and even excels.

As harmony is praised, the employees are treated as the most precious assets in the company. This is in line with the traditional Confucian approach to leadership in which the sage believed that the proper management of a state is to satisfy the needs of its people first. As such, and influenced by the strong familial relationship in the company, the Chinese TQM company would view employee satisfaction as a prerequisite for customer satisfaction. Conventional TQM principles as seen in most Japanese and American companies have put foremost emphasis on customer satisfaction. It is the other way around in the Chinese TQM company. First create satisfied employees, then satisfied customers. Employee satisfaction is thus greatly influenced by the hierarchical relationship in the organization, the father-like figure of the leader, and the harmonious familial atmosphere in the organization. This is in line with Hui and Tan's (1996: 371) argument that when respect is given, the Chinese perceive their personal worth as being reinstated in the group and this leads to increased job satisfaction and work productivity. Some concrete examples of maintaining a harmonious human relationship are appealing. For example, the elimination of the Western 'one champion' system in QCC contests is an

extremely good example of maintaining harmony, and more importantly, face.

At the extrinsic level of creating employee satisfaction, monetary
rewards play an important role in enhancing employees to pay extra
efforts. Very much different from the Japanese companies whose QCCs
are mostly voluntary, Chinese QCCs usually have to be encouraged
with some monetary rewards. As the Chinese are famous for being pragmatic and situation oriented, this is not difficult to understand. For
example, Cheng and Chan (1999) reported that Chinese workers in
practicing TQM are frequently more motivated by what they call technological factors, referring to factual and visible work improvement and
personal career development. The authors also cited the findings of
Chau and Chan (1984) and Wang (1992) which indicated that good pay
and achievement oriented rewards are highly acknowledged by Chinese
workers. On the other hand, Kanji *et al.* (1995) found that building
teamwork rather than the bonus system is a major contributor towards
quality motivation for Japanese and Korean workers.

What is important here is the ability of the father-like leader to play
around the thin and delicate line separating extrinsic and intrinsic
rewards. At suitable times, mandatory task forces are assigned to solve
problems. At other times, employees are encouraged to provide simple
suggestions on workplace improvement with small monetary rewards.
Winning circles in QCC contests are given monetary rewards as well as
personal acknowledgments by the top leaders. To grasp the psychology
of the Chinese employees, a photo taken with the top leader is much
worthier than actual cash rewards. The leader in the Chinese TQM
company must be skillful in truly understanding what the employees
need at different times and on different occasions.

Interdependence plays an important role in customer relationships.
These intimate and caring relationships are best described by the Chinese
sayings so often mentioned by the managers in the companies interviewed, for example, 'all men within four seas are brothers', 'the mountain
and water will meet one day', 'we are all on the same boat', and so on.
Thus, relationships are aimed to be maintained at the long-term with
the best efforts exerted by, for example, allowing generous concessions
when possible and giving technical advice to customers so as to reap
mutual benefits.

All in all, the relationships between Chinese cultural values and TQM
principles are so complex and intimate that it is actually impossible to
describe each and every aspect in full. Further descriptions would probably render the Chinese-style TQM as magnificent and invulnerable

as the Japanese-style management which was once misunderstood. It is a fact that the TQM journey for the Chinese firms, especially those in mainland China, is still long and winding. Researchers such as Wacker (1986), Green (1990), Zhao *et al.* (1995), and Yeung and Chan (1999) have pointed out that many Chinese manufacturing firms do suffer from serious drawbacks when compared to their Western counterparts in terms of TQM implementation. For example, under-educated workers who come from remote rural areas in China are often difficult to be properly trained. Furthermore, unenlightened management staff lacking a modern approach to quality management is also a common problem. Nevertheless, according to the findings of Yeung and Chan (1999), successful TQM firms in China found Chinese cultural values to be positive towards TQM implementation while many firms which were unsuccessful in implementing TQM found some Chinese cultural values to be barriers instead (Chiu, 1999). Thus, it is again a matter of whether the Chinese companies are able to realize the two-sided nature of Chinese values, whether they can fully integrate the positive side of Confucian values with TQM and to gradually wipe out the negative side of the coin as what has been experienced in the case of Jinling.

It is indeed true that the Chinese TQM company does strive to maintain the image of a big and harmonious family. But when it comes to pragmatic situations such as the repercussions from the recent Asian economic turmoil, tradeoffs between pragmatism and morality do exist as difficult decisions for the Chinese managers. External influences as such represent painful experiences not only for the Chinese managers. These rather represent universal problems. What is important in the present study is to point out that the Chinese-style TQM does have its own strengths and weaknesses. In order to be successful in this turbulent age, it is important for one to realize his or her own unique cultural heritage and to make full use of it so as to achieve a satisfactory fusion effect with TQM principles. It is likely to be a worthwhile exercise in determining one's own strengths and weaknesses in all sorts of daily activities, not to mention only commercial endeavors. As Confucius once said in the Analects, 'Not to cultivate virtue, not to review what is learned, not to do the righteous though having heard of it, not to rectify what is not good – these things are what I worry about'.

The discussion ends here with a quotation taken from Shenkar and von Glinow's (1994: 59) attempt to pinpoint the unconscious inclination of Western researchers to induce models from their own contextual circumstances. ' ... for Confucius, administrative work was an activity of such paramount importance that it has been translated into a very explicit prescription on organization and management which is nowhere to be found in Western philosophies'. Indeed, the study of cultural values in the context of managerial endeavors is nonetheless a mine of treasures still to be uncovered.

8
Summary and Conclusion

This chapter closes the present study with some further thoughts. The general orientation of the study is firstly restated, followed by a brief summary of the findings. Then the weaknesses and implications of the study are mentioned. Finally, some recommendations for further research are given.

General orientation of the study

The study argues that TQM, when implemented in a certain cultural context, leads to a fusion between the underlying cultural values and the fundamental TQM principles, thus creating a culture-specific TQM. This culture-specific TQM has its own ways of operation and manifestation leading to the fundamental objectives of quality improvement. Following the Parsonian framework, an organization's culture functions as a sub-value system largely influenced by the super-ordinate value system. Total quality management itself as a transcendent culture has abundant room to work within the unique quality climate of the organization. Whether TQM will sustain or fail relies largely on how it fuses with the quality climate, which is in turn influenced by the national culture setting. In other words, there is no pre-packaged TQM applicable to all organizations worldwide. The implementation of TQM has to be culture specific. Although some cultural values may appear more in line with TQM principles while others may not, it does not mean that an organization can simply use TQM to transform its culture. Rather, TQM and the respective organizational climate must fuse together, absorbing each other mutually. Otherwise we shall be left with no basis in distinguishing why American, Japanese, as well as Chinese companies which are embedded in cultural values so distinct can still excel in TQM endeavors.

Many researchers have proposed theories dealing with the creation of an organizational culture positive towards the implementation of TQM activities. However, very few have ever linked the study of TQM with national culture in spite of anecdotal evidence that such an impact is clear. The present study makes its share of contribution by operationalizing the theoretical variables of national culture, organizational quality climate, and quality management system implementation. This has led to the development of an explicit and comprehensive model for explaining the inter-relationships among cultural values and quality management elements.

Summary of findings

This section of the chapter summarizes the findings of each major step of the study namely, the TQM survey, the CCV survey, the structural equation model, and the case studies. After these, an integrated summary is presented.

To assess the situation of TQM implementation, a modified version of the Quality and Productivity Self-Assessment Guide for Defense Organizations Version 1.0 (DoD, 1992) was administered to a total of 385 ISO 9000 certified Chinese companies operating in Hong Kong, Taiwan, and mainland China. Factor analysis revealed 11 underlying factors which are: (1) commitment to quality; (2) unity of purpose; (3) harmonious system; (4) communication; (5) organizational planning and evaluation; (6) organizational flexibility and employee orientation; (7) training and information analysis; (8) teamwork; (9) scientific approach; (10) customer satisfaction; and (11) workplace *kaizen*. These factors assembled around four major quality dimensions namely: (1) quality climate (QC); (2) quality processes (QP); (3) quality methods (QM); and (4) quality results (QR). A comprehensive literature review showed that critical TQM elements basically resemble these factors.

To uncover major value dimensions of Chinese culture, the Chinese cultural value inventory developed by Yau (1994) was employed. Confirmatory factor analysis revealed that the original 12 factors theoretically anchored on Kluckhohn and Strodtbeck's (1961) value orientation framework are basically representative of Chinese cultural values. The 12 values include: (1) harmony with nature; (2) *yuarn*; (3) abasement; (4) situation orientation; (5) respect for authority; (6) interdependence; (7) group orientation; (8) face; (9) continuity; (10) past time orientation; (11) doctrine of the mean; and (12) harmony with others. The model is consistent with the value orientation framework encompassing the man to nature orientation, man-himself orientation, relational orientation, time orientation, and personal activity orientation.

A structural equation model explaining the inter-relationships among the four quality dimensions and Chinese cultural values was then postulated. The four quality dimensions took the form of a process-type model with QC as the input variables, QP and QM as the process variables, and QR as the output variable. This quality management model is in line with the ARS theory of quality management (Anderson *et al.*, 1994). The inclusion of Chinese cultural values (CV) represents a refined four-proposition framework by stressing the importance of the underlying values of organizational members.

The proposed structural model incorporating the influence of CV on the four-variable quality management model with QC acting as an intermediary was tested. The minimized discrepancy function and other fit indices indicated a good model fit. To further validate the model, an alternative model was postulated with CV having direct effects on QP, QM, and QR. This model was rejected given that no statistically significant influences were exerted by CV on any of these three quality variables.

The influence of Chinese cultural values on TQM has been statistically proven. However, the question, in what ways or forms do such relationships function in reality, cannot be easily answered. Therefore, three case studies were presented with the hope of using real life examples to qualitatively support the statistical findings.

Three Chinese companies, one operating in Hong Kong, and the other two in mainland China, were depicted. In general, it was learnt through interviews that the company leaders are most instrumental in instilling an organizational climate positive towards TQM. This is frequently based on personal mottoes of life, which in turn are based on traditional Chinese values. It was also found that a harmonious and familial relationship is highly valued. Success is a matter of integrating a systematic management system with the Chinese approach of human relations emphasizing trust and collective harmony. Furthermore, a re-emphasis on traditional Confucian values has recently been stressed by company leaders due to China's gradual political reform. Nevertheless, the abuse of traditional values has to be inhibited by implementing a systematic management approach. In particular, the adaptiveness and situation orientation of the Chinese people were found to be highly helpful towards this end.

After schematically mapping back the remarks and statements given by the interviewees with the Chinese cultural values identified in the model, a deeper understanding of how these values are manifested in

TQM activities was obtained. In order to describe the salient characteristics of the Chinese-style TQM model, a schematic framework encompassing all quantitative and qualitative findings was developed. Some of these characteristics are summarized here.

1. The organizational climate represents a fusion between the Confucian paternalistic and hierarchical relationships and the participative management style as advocated in TQM. The essence is to use the former to act as the boundary within which the latter works so as to maintain a harmonious family-like organization.

2. Organizational leaders cannot simply provide tacit spiritual guidance. Rather, they are 'down to earth'. They have to fully involve and participate in day-to-day activities in order to demonstrate real life examples of the virtuous father-like figure. The realization of personal mottoes in life provides the key ingredients of the meaning of corporate existence.

3. The Western quantum leap or pure innovation approach is not congruent with Chinese cultural values. Rather, the emphasis is on adapting and refining foreign technologies so as to result in a unique system. Thus, the institutional arrangements of good Western management practices are highly acknowledged in the building of a well-structured system while it is contextualized by underlying Chinese values.

4. Education is highly praised. Multiple-skill training is emphasized and must be assessed periodically through examinations. This brings about visible expectations and achievements in congruence with Chinese pragmatism.

5. Collective rather than individual talent is encouraged. A contingent application of both monetary and intrinsic rewards to enhance group participation is vital. The Western individualistic 'one champion' approach nor the Japanese-style voluntarism are directly applicable.

6. The priority of the company is to provide employee satisfaction which will in turn lead to customer satisfaction. Familism is extended out of the organizational boundaries to the customers and trading partners.

Implications and weaknesses of the study and further research

To the field of quality management, the theoretical contribution of this study lies in the development of an explicit and comprehensive model for explaining the inter-relationships among national cultural values and quality management elements.

Due to rapid globalization, national differences in terms of the 'hard' aspects like technology are diminishing. In order to create unique competitiveness, there is a need for TQM practitioners to shift from the traditional universalistic approach to a culturalist approach. This paradigmatic shift is essential for the better understanding and management of today's organizational phenomena. Without a thorough emic analysis of one's cultural system, hybridization of different management approaches will be impossible. As argued in Chapter 2, there is indeed a need to theorize TQM from a more open, socio-cultural, specific, and derived etic approach. It is hoped that the perspective of this study has taken a small step in filling up the lacuna of TQM research often labeled as atheoretical and ethnocentric.

Most theories on organizational climate related to TQM are based on Western psychological and social processes. The present research is among the first to relate Chinese cultural values with TQM following an emic and derived etic approach. With the Chinese economy representing one of the hottest area of research in business management today, the present study has actually presented timely information and an alternative to the Western or Japanese TQM literature.

Practically speaking, TQM has never been a miraculous drug for companies wishing to engage in quality improvement. The successful implementation of TQM for visible results requires time and effort, and most important of all, adaptation to the local cultural context. The inter-relationships among the elements in the model and the schematic framework of the Chinese TQM model could provide useful information for the TQM practitioner. The explicit examples of leadership style, group activities, and customer orientation, for instance, should contribute practical value. As such, a better understanding of the cultural values relevant to TQM activities helps to formulate better strategies to model one's own TQM activities. In other words, practitioners need a thorough self-reflection before adoption of a particular systematic management approach. Total quality management is essentially people-oriented management. For the Chinese people to succeed in today's global competition, understanding their own culture stemming from a civilization of over four thousand years is an essential prerequisite.

A major limitation of the present study is the lack of more in-depth study on how the TQM companies in the three Chinese regions differ, but achieving the same quality results. The study has concentrated more on the aspect of commonalities but less on differences. Delineating these differences is warranted because the three Chinese regions do demonstrate different social, political, and cultural background. Should sufficient samples be obtained from the three regions, then three separate structural models could be compared. As the culture-specific TQM model is believed to exist in different cultures, the eventual objective is to conduct cross-cultural studies so as to identify similarities and differences among different culture-specific TQM models. This series of further research will greatly contribute to the existing literature of cross-cultural management theory.

The call for larger samples above is indeed important because the low response rate in the present study may lead to non-response bias. Problems with construct validity of Chinese cultural value were also encountered. In particular, the lack of multiple measurements for some values such as past time orientation is a drawback hoped to be remedied in future redesign of the CCV scale. Also, there is a need to reassess certain Chinese cultural values given the trend of changing values within mainland China, not to mention other overseas Chinese regions. Furthermore, the use of multiple measurement scales for Chinese values as well as TQM dimensions should prove useful in future replication studies.

Concerning the qualitative case studies performed in the present study, should resources allow, more sophisticated techniques such as ethnography and other advanced qualitative research methods should be used. There is today an abundance of well-documented texts on the formal procedures of various sociological research methods such as grounded theory which is highly suitable for organization and management research (for example, Strauss and Corbin, 1990). Also, the number of companies interviewed remained relatively small for the purpose of achieving generalizability. More qualitative studies on a larger number of companies providing more interesting and in-depth stories are called for.

Throughout the study, the abandonment of a universalistic, ethnocentric, and manageralistic approach to TQM and TQM research has been advocated. It must be mentioned here that recently there has been a trend to evaluate TQM from a critical science or post-modern approach. This has probably started with a special issue of the *Journal of Organizational Change Management* on TQM in 1993. For example, Boje and Winsor (1993) critically pointed out that the hidden agenda of TQM is the resurrection of Taylorism, which can have dysfunctional effects if improperly managed. In the same issue, Steingard and Fitzgibbons (1993) published their post-modern deconstruction of TQM. These attempts were followed by Wilkinson and Willmott's (1995) edited volume and

Wilkinson *et al.*'s (1998) recent presentation of case studies as well as critical evaluations of TQM. In a similar vein, TQM viewed from post-modern perspectives such as power and authority (Knights and McCabe, 1999), discourse and transformation (Xu, 1999), representation and difference (De Cock, 1998) are seen to continually emerge. Indeed, the period of 'the blossom of a hundred flowers' has just started for TQM research.

References

Abo, T. (ed.) (1994). *Hybrid Factory: The Japanese Production System in the United States*. New York: Oxford University Press.

Adam, E., Hershauer, J. and Ruch, W.A. (1981). *Productivity and Quality*. Englewood Cliffs, NJ: Prentice-Hall.

Adler, N.J. (1983). 'A typology of management studies involving culture', *Journal of International Business Studies*, 14(2): 29–47.

Allan, J. (1998). 'Perspectives on research in quality management', *Total Quality Management*, 9(4, 5): S1–S5.

Amemiya, Y. and Anderson, T.W. (1990). 'Asymptotic chi-square tests for a large class of factor analysis model', *The Annals of Statistics*, 18: 1453–63.

Anderson, J.C., Rungtusanatham, M. and Schroeder, R.G. (1994). 'A theory of quality management underlying the Deming management method', *Academy of Management Review*, 19(3): 472–509.

Anderson, J.C., Rungtusanatham, M., Schroeder, R.G. and Devaraj, S. (1995). 'A path analytic model of a theory of quality management underlying the Deming management method: Preliminary empirical findings', *Decision Sciences*, 26(5): 637–58.

APO (1997). *Productivity Statistics: Productivity Indexes and Levels in APO Member Countries*. Tokyo: Asian Productivity Organization.

Arbuckle, J. (1997). *Amos User's Guide*. Chicago: Smallwaters Corporation.

Bagozzi, R.P. (1980). *Causal Models in Marketing*. New York: John Wiley & Sons.

Bem, D.J. (1970). *Beliefs, Attitudes, and Human Affairs*. Belmont, CA: Brooks.

Bentler, P.M. and Bonett, D.G. (1980). 'Significance tests and goodness of fit in the analysis of covariance structure', *Psychological Bulletin*, 88(3): 588–606.

Berry, J.W. (1969). 'On cross-cultural comparability', *International Journal of Psychology*, 4(2): 119–28.

Berry, J.W. (1990). 'Imposed etics, emics, and derived etics: Their conceptual and operational states in cross-cultural psychology', in T.N. Headland, K.L. Pike and H. Harris (eds), *Emics and Etics*. London: Sage.

Berry, J.W., Poortinga, Y.H., Segall, M.H. and Dasen, P.R. (1992). *Cross-Cultural Psychology: Research and Applications*. New York: Cambridge University Press.

Beyer, J.M., Ashmos, D.P. and Osborn, R.N. (1996). Contrasts in easing TQM: Mechanistic vs. organic ideology and implementation. Unpublished manuscript.

Black, S. and Porter, L. (1996). 'Identification of the critical factors of TQM', *Decision Sciences*, 27(1): 1–21.

Blalock, H.M., Jr. (1961). *Causal Inferences in Non-experimental Research*. New York: W.W. Norton & Co.

Bohrnstedt, G.W. and Knoke, D. (1988). *Statistics for Social Data Analysis*. Second edition. Itasca, IL: F.E. Peacock Publishers.

Boje, D.M. and Winsor, R.D. (1993). 'The resurrection of Taylorism: Total quality management's hidden agenda', *Journal of Organizational Change Management*, 6(4): 57–70.

Bond, M.H. (1988). 'Finding universal dimensions of individual variations in multi-cultural studies: The Rokeach and Chinese value surveys', *Journal of Personality and Social Psychology*, 55(6): 1009–15.

Bond, M.H. (1996). 'Chinese Values', in M.H. Bond (ed.), *The Handbook of Chinese Psychology*. New York: Oxford University Press.

Bond, M.H. and Hwang, K.K. (1986). 'The social psychology of Chinese people', in M. Bond (ed.), *The Psychology of the Chinese People*. New York: Oxford University Press.

Bounds, G., Yorks, L., Adams, M. and Ranney, G. (1994). *Beyond Total Quality Management*. Singapore: McGraw-Hill.

Boyer, R. (1998). 'Hybridization and models of production: Geography, history, and theory', in R. Boyer, E. Charron, U. Jurgens, and S. Tolliday (eds), *Between Imitation and Innovation: The Transfer and Hybridization of Productive Models in the International Automobile Industry*. New York: Oxford University Press.

Bright, K. and Cooper, C.L. (1993). 'Organizational culture and the management of quality: Towards a new framework', *Journal of Managerial Psychology*, 8(6): 21–7.

Brislin, R.W. (1980). 'Translation and content analysis of oral and written material', in H.C. Triandis and J.W. Berry (eds), *Handbook of Cross-Cultural Psychology Volume 1*. Boston, MA: Allyn and Bacon.

Brocka, B. and Brocka, M.S. (1992). *Quality Management: Implementing the Best Ideas of the Masters*. Homewood, IL: Richard D. Irwin.

Browne, M.W. (1984). 'Asymptotic distribution-free methods for the analysis of covariance structures', *British Journal of Mathematics and Statistical Psychology*, 37: 62–83.

Browne, M.W. and Shapiro, A. (1988). 'Robustness of normal theory methods in the analysis of linear latent variate models', *British Journal of Mathematics and Statistical Psychology*, 41: 193–208.

Bureau of Business Practice (1992). *ISO 9000: Handbook of Quality Standards and Compliance*. Englewood Cliffs, NJ: Prentice Hall.

Cameron, K. and Sine, W. (1999). 'A framework for organizational quality culture', *Quality Management Journal*, 6(4): 7–25.

Chapman, R. (1998). 'Introduction', in *Total-Quality-Culture, an internet discussion forum* (http://www.mailbase.ac.uk/lists/total-quality-culture/).

Chau, A. and Chan, G. (1984). 'A study of job satisfaction of workers in local factories of Chinese, Western, and Japanese ownership', *The Hong Kong Manager*, September, pp. 9–17.

Chen, W.H. (1997) 'The human side of total quality management in Taiwan: leadership and human resource management', *International Journal of Quality and Reliability Management*, 14(1): 24–45.

Chen, W.H. and Lu, R.S.Y (1998). 'A Chinese approach to quality transformation', *International Journal of Quality and Reliability Management*, 15(1): 72–84.

Cheng, J.P. (1990). *Confucius as a Teacher: Philosophy of Confucius with Special Reference to its Educational Implications*. Beijing: Foreign Language Press.

Cheng, T.C. (1996). 'Survey report: Hong Kong', in T. Umeda (ed.), *TQM Practices in Asia-Pacific Firms*. Tokyo: Asian Productivity Organization.

Cheng, T.K. and Chan, S.F.F. (1999). 'Quality motivation in China: Humanistic and technological', *Total Quality Management*, 10(7): 967–78.

Cheung, F.M. (1996). 'The assessment of psychopathology in Chinese societies', in M.H. Bond (ed.), *The Handbook of Chinese Psychology*. New York: Oxford University Press.

Child, J. (1994). *Management in China During the Age of Reform*. New York: Cambridge University Press.

Chiles, T.H. and Choi, T.Y. (2000). 'Theorizing TQM: An Austrian and evolutionary economics interpretation', *Journal of Management Studies*, 37(2): 185–212.

Chiu, R.K. (1999). 'Employee involvement in a TQM program: problems in Chinese firms in Hong Kong', *Managerial Auditing Journal*, 14(1): 8–11.

Choi, T.Y. and Liker, J.K. (1995). 'Bringing Japanese continuous improvement approaches to U.S. manufacturing: The roles of process orientation and communications', *Decision Sciences*, 26(5): 589–620.

Chu, G.C. (1967). 'Sex differences in persuability of factors among Chinese', *International Journal of Psychology*, 2: 283–8.

Clegg, S., Dunphy, D. and Redding, S.G. (1986). 'Organization and management in East Asia', in S. Clegg, D. Dunphy, and S.G. Redding (eds), *The Enterprise & Management in East Asia*. Hong Kong: University of Hong Kong.

Cochran, W.G. (1952). 'The χ^2 test of goodness of fit', *Annals of Mathematical Statistics*, 23: 315–45.

Crittenden, K.S. (1996). 'Causal attribution process among the Chinese', in M.H. Bond (ed.), *The Handbook of Chinese Psychology*. New York: Oxford University Press.

Cronbach, L.J. and Meehl, P.E. (1955). 'Construct validity in psychological tests', *Psychological Bulletin*, 52: 282–302.

Crosby, P.B. (1979). *Quality is Free*. New York: McGraw-Hill.

Crosby, P.B. (1986). *Quality Without Tears*. New York: McGraw-Hill.

Curkovic, S. and Handfield, R.B. (1996). 'Use of ISO 9000 and Baldrige Award criteria in supplier quality evaluation', *International Journal of Purchasing and Materials Management*, Spring, pp. 2–11.

Curkovic, S. and Pagell, M. (1999). 'A critical examination of the ability of ISO 9000 certification to lead to a competitive advantage', *Journal of Quality Management*, 4(1): 51–67.

Dale, B.G. (1991). 'Starting on the road to success', *TQM Magazine*, 3(2): 125–8.

Dale, B.G. (1994). 'Japanese total quality control', in B.G. Dale (ed.), *Managing Quality*. Second edition. Hertfordshire: Prentice Hall Europe.

Dale, B.G. and Boaden, R.J. (1994). 'A generic framework for managing quality', in B.G. Dale (ed.), *Managing Quality*. Second edition. Hertfordshire: Prentice Hall Europe.

Dale, B.G., Boaden, R.J. and Lascelles, D.M. (1994). 'Total quality management: An overview', in B.G. Dale (ed.), *Managing Quality*. Second edition. Hertfordshire: Prentice Hall Europe.

Dale, B.G., Lascelles, D.M. and Plunkett, J.J. (1990). 'The process of total quality management', in B.G. Dale and J.J. Plunkett (eds), *Managing Quality*. Hertfordshire: Philip Allan.

de Bary, W.T. (1988). *East Asian Civilizations: A Dialogue in Five Stages*. Cambridge, MA: Harvard University Press.

De Cock, C. (1998). ' "It seems to fill my head with ideas": A few thoughts on postmodernism, TQM, and BPR', *Journal of Management Inquiry*, 7(2): 144–53.

De Cock, C. and Hipkin, I. (1997). 'TQM and BPR: Beyond the beyond myth', *Journal of Management Studies*, 34(5): 659–75.

De Mente, B.L. (1991). *Behind the Japanese Bow*. Lincolnwood, IL: Passport Books.

Deal, T. and Kennedy, A. (1988). *Corporate Cultures: The Rites and Rituals of Corporate Life*. Harmondsworth: Penguin.

Dean, J.W., Jr. and Bowen, D.E. (1994). 'Management theory and total quality: Improving research and practice through theory development', *Academy of Management Review*, 19(3): 392–419.

Deming, W.E. (1986). *Out of the Crisis*. Cambridge, MA: Massachusetts Institute of Technology.

Denzin, N. (1989). *The Research Act*. Englewood Cliffs, NJ: Prentice-Hall.

DeVor, R.E., Chang, T.H. and Sutherland, J. (1992). *Statistical Quality Design and Control: Contemporary Concepts and Methods*. New York: Macmillan Publishing Co.

DoD (1990). *Quality and Productivity Self-Assessment Guide for Defense Organizations*. Washington DC: US Department of Defense.

DoD (1992). *Quality and Productivity Self-Assessment Guide for Defense Organizations Version 1.0*. Washington DC: US Department of Defense.

Douglas, T.J. and Judge, W.Q., Jr. (2001). 'Total quality management implementation and competitive advantage: The role of structural control and exploration', *Academy of Management Journal*, 44(1): 158–169.

Dyer, W.G. and Wilkins, A.L. (1991). 'Better stories, not better constructs, to generate better theory: A rejoinder to Eisenhardt', *Academy of Management Review*, 16(3): 613–19.

Efron, B. and Tibshirani, R. (1986). 'Bootstrap methods for standard errors, confidence intervals, and other measures of statistical accuracy', *Statistical Science*, 1: 54–74.

Emery, F. (1978). 'A concern for quality', *Human Futures*, Summer, pp. 100–104.

Eisenhardt, K.M. (1989). 'Building theories from case study research', *Academy of Management Review*, 14(4): 532–50.

Eisenhardt, K.M. (1991). 'Better stories and better constructs: The case for rigor and comparative logic', *Academy of Management Review*, 16(3): 620–7.

Fan, Y. (1998). 'The transfer of Western management to China: Context, content and constraints', *Management Learning*, 29(2): 201–21.

Feigenbaum, A.V. (1991). *Total Quality Control*. New York: McGraw-Hill.

Fishbein, M. and Ajzen, I. (1975). *Belief, Attitude, Intention and Behavior: An Introduction to Theory and Research*. Reading, MA: Addison Wesley.

Flynn, B.B., Schroeder, R.G. and Sakakibara, S. (1994). 'A framework for quality management research and an associated measurement instrument', *Journal of Operations Management*, 11(4): 339–66.

Flynn, B.B., Sakakibara, S. and Schroeder, R.G. (1995). 'Relationship between JIT and TQM: Practices and performance', *Academy of Management Journal*, 38(5): 1325–60.

Fröhner, K.D. and Iwata, K. (1996). 'Evaluating designing principles of Japanese production systems', *International Journal of Production Economics*, 46–7: 211–17.

Gabrenya, W.K., Jr. and Hwang, K.K. (1996). 'Chinese social interaction: harmony and hierarchy on the good earth', in M.H. Bond (ed.), *The Handbook of Chinese Psychology*. New York: Oxford University Press.

Gao, G., Ting, S.T. and Gudykunst, W. (1996). 'Chinese communication processes', in M.H. Bond (ed.), *The Handbook of Chinese Psychology*. New York: Oxford University Press.

Garvin, D.A. (1983). 'Quality on the line', *Harvard Business Review*, 61(5): 65–75.

Garvin, D.A. (1984). 'Japanese quality management', *Columbia Journal of World Business*, 19(3): 3–12.

Garvin, D.A. (1986). 'Quality problems, policies, and attitudes in the United States and Japan: An exploratory study', *Academy of Management Journal*, 29(4): 653–73.

Garvin, D.A. (1988). *Managing Quality: The Strategic and Competitive Edge*. New York: The Free Press.

Ghauri, P., Grønhaug, K. and Kristianslund, I. (1995). *Research Methods in Business Studies: A Practical Guide*. Hertfordshire: Prentice Hall International (UK).

Gitlow, H.S. (1994). 'Total quality management in the United States and Japan', *APO Productivity Journal*, Winter, 93–4: 3–27.

Glaser, B. and Strauss, A. (1967). *The Discovery of Grounded Theory: Strategies of Qualitative Research*. Chicago: Aldine.

Goh, T.N. (1993). 'Taguchi methods: some technical, cultural and pedagogical perspectives', *Quality and Reliability Engineering International*, 9: 185–202.

Goetsch, D.L. and Davis, S. (1994). *Introduction to Total Quality: Quality, Productivity, Competitiveness*. New York: Macmillan College Publishing Co.

Goodwin, R. and Tang, C.S.K. (1996). 'Chinese personal relationships', in M.H. Bond (ed.), *The Handbook of Chinese Psychology*. New York: Oxford University Press.

Grandzol, J.R. and Gershon, M. (1998). 'A survey instrument for standardizing TQM modeling research', *International Journal of Quality Science*, 3(1): 80–105.

Grant, R.M., Shani, R. and Krishnan, P. (1994). 'TQM's challenge to management theory and practice', *Sloan Management Review*, Winter, pp. 25–35.

Green, K. (1990). 'The uphill climb towards quality', *The China Business Review*, 17(3): 10–13.

Guilford, J.P. (1959). *Personality*. New York: McGraw-Hill.

Gulliksen, H. and Tukey, J.W. (1958). 'Reliability for the law of comparative judgment', *Psychometrika*, 23: 95–110.

Hackman, J.R. and Wageman, R. (1995). 'Total quality management: empirical, conceptual, and practical issues', *Administrative Science Quarterly*, 40: 309–342.

Hair, J.F., Anderson, R.E., Tatham, R.L. and Black, W.C. (1998). *Multivariate Data Analysis*. Fifth edition. Upper Saddle River, NJ: Simon & Shuster Company.

Hall, R.W. (1983). *Zero Inventories*. Homewood, IL: Dow Jones-Irwin.

Hammer, M. and Champy, J. (1994). *Reengineering the Corporation: A Manifesto for Business Revolution*. New York: Harper & Row.

Hampden-Turner, C. and Trompenaars, A. (1993). *The Seven Cultures of Capitalism*. New York: Double Day.

Handfield, R.B. and Melnyk, S.A. (1998). 'The scientific theory-building process: A primer using the case of TQM', *Journal of Operations Management*, 16: 321–39.

Hansen, T. (2001). 'Quality in the marketplace: A theoretical and empirical investigation', *European Management Journal*, 19(2): 203–11.

Hansen, W. (1994). *Lecture notes for ISO/DIN/DGQ Regional Training Seminar for Quality System Auditors*. HC Hansen Consult.

Harris, C.R. (1995). 'The evolution of quality management: An overview of the TQM literature', *Canadian Journal of Administrative Sciences*, 12(2): 95–103.

Hasegawa, H. (1998). 'Japanese global strategies in Europe and the formation of regional markets', in H. Hasegawa and G.D. Hook (eds), *Japanese Business Management: Restructuring for Low Growth and Globalization*. London: Routledge.

Hellersberg, E.F. (1953). 'Visual perception and spatial organizations: A study of performance on the Horn-Hellersberg Test by Chinese subjects', in M. Mead and R. Metraux (eds), *The Study of Chinese at a Distance*. Chicago: University of Chicago Press.

Hildebrandt, S., Kristensen, K., Kanji, G. and Dahlgaard, J.J. (1991). 'Quality culture and TQM', *Total Quality Management*, 2(1): 1–14.

Hiniker, P.J. (1969). 'Chinese reactions to forced compliments: Dissonance reduction or national character'? *Journal of Social Psychology*, 77: 157–76.

HKQAA (1996). *Buyer's Guide July 1996*. Hong Kong: Hong Kong Quality Assurance Agency.

Hofstede, G. (1980). *Culture's Consequences: International Differences in Work-Related Values*. London: Sage.

Hofstede, G. (1991). *Cultures and organizations: Software of the Mind*. London: McGraw-Hill International.

Hofstede, G. and Bond, M.H. (1988). 'The Confucian connection: From cultural roots to economic growth', *Organizational Dynamics*, 16(4): 4–21.

Hoyle, R.H. (1995). 'The structural equation modeling approach: Basic concepts and fundamental issues', in R.H. Hoyle (ed.), *Structural Equation Modeling: Concepts, Issues, and Applications*. Thousand Oaks, CA: Sage.

Hoyle, R.H. and Panter, A.T. (1995). 'Writing about structural equation models', in R.H. Hoyle (ed.), *Structural Equation Modeling: Concepts, Issues, and Applications*. Thousand Oaks, CA: Sage.

Hu, H.C. (1944). 'The Chinese concept of "face" ', *American Anthropologist*, 46: 45–64.

Hu, L.T. and Bentler, P.M. (1995). 'Evaluating model fit', in R.H. Hoyle (ed.), *Structural Equation Modeling: Concepts, Issues, and Applications*. Thousand Oaks, CA: Sage.

Huang, H.C., Hwang, K.K. and Ko, Y.H. (1983). 'Life stress, attribution style, social support and depression among university students (in Chinese)', *Acta Psychologia Taiwanica*, 25: 31–47.

Hui, C.H. and Tan, K.C. (1996). 'Employee motivation and attitudes in the Chinese workplace', in M.H. Bond (ed.), *The Handbook of Chinese Psychology*. New York: Oxford University Press.

Hwang, K.K. (1987). 'Face and favor: The Chinese power game', *American Journal of Sociology*, 92(4): 944–74.

Iizuka, Y. (1996). 'Integrating ISO 9000 with Japan's TQM', *APO Productivity Journal*, Winter, pp. 3–23.

Imai, M. (1991). *Kaizen: The Key to Japan's Competitive Success*. Singapore: McGraw-Hill International.

Inkeles, A. and Levinson, D.J. (1954). 'National character: The study of modal personality and sociocultural systems', in G. Lindzey (ed.), *Handbook of Social Psychology*. Reading, MA: Addison Wesley.

ISO (1994a). *ISO Standards Compendium: ISO 9000 Quality Management*. Geneva: International Organization for Standardization.

ISO (1994b). *Compatible Technology Worldwide*. Geneva: International Organization for Standardization.

ISO (2000). *The ISO Survey of ISO 9000 and ISO 14000 Certificates: Ninth Cycle*. Geneva: International Organization for Standardization.

ISO (2001a). ISO 9000/ISO 14000: Quality management principles. *ISO Online* (http://www.iso.ch/iso/en/iso9000-14000/iso9000/qmp.html).

ISO (2001b). Transition to the ISO 9000: 2000 series: The year 2000 revisions of ISO 9001 and ISO 9004. *ISO Online* (http://isotc176sc2.elysium-ltd.net/Year%202000%20revisions.html).

ISO 9000 News. January, 1994.

Ishikawa, K. (1964). *Hinshitsu Kanri Nyumon*. Tokyo: JUSE Press.

Ishikawa, K. (1985). *What is Total Quality Control? The Japanese Way*. Englewood Cliffs, NJ: Prentice-Hall.

Ishikawa, K. (1990). *Introduction to Quality Control*. Tokyo: 3A Corporation.

Japan Productivity Center for Socio-Economic Development (1994). In Pursuit of Creative Management in the Context of Globalization. Consultation paper for managerial reform, November.

Jenner, R.A., Herbert, L., Appell, A. and Baack, J. (1998). 'Using quality management for cultural transformation of Chinese state enterprises: A case study', *Journal of Quality Management*, 3(2): 193–210.

Jöreskog, K.G. (1969). 'A general approach to confirmatory maximum likelihood factor analysis', *Psychometrika*, 32: 443–82.

Jöreskog, K.G. (1993). 'Testing structural equation models', in K.A. Bollen, and J.S. Long (eds), *Testing Structural Equation Models*. Thousand Oaks, CA: Sage.

Juran, J.M. (1951). *Quality Control Handbook*. New York: McGraw-Hill.

Juran, J.M. (1988). *Juran on Planning for Quality*. New York: The Free Press.

Juran, J.M. (1989). *Juran on Leadership for Quality: An Executive Handbook*. New York: The Free Press.

Juran, J.M. (1992). *Juran on Quality by Design: The New Steps for Planning Quality into Goods and Services*. New York: The Free Press.

Juran, J.M. (1995). *Managerial Breakthrough: The Classic Book on Improving Management Performance*. New York: McGraw-Hill.

Kaiser, H.F. (1960). 'The application of electronic computers to factor analysis', *Educational and Psychological Measurement*, 20: 141–51.

Kanji, G.K. (1990). 'Total quality management: the second industrial revolution', *Total Quality Management*, 1(1): 3–12.

Kanji, G.K. (1994). 'Total quality management and statistical understanding', *Total Quality Management*, 5(3): 105–114.

Kanji, G.K. (1996). 'Implementation and pitfalls of total quality management', *Total Quality Management*, 7(3): 331–43.

Kanji, G.K. (1998). 'An innovative approach to make ISO 9000 standards more effective', *Total Quality Management*, 9(1): 67–78.

Kanji, G.K., Kristensen, K. and Dahlgaard, J.J. (1995). 'Quality motivation', *Total Quality Management*, 6(4): 427–34.

Kanji, G.K. and Yui, H. (1997). 'Total quality culture', *Total Quality Management*, 8(6): 417–28.

Kano, N. (1994). 'TQM in Japan: A retrospective and prospective outlook', *APO Productivity Journal*, Winter, 93–4: 3–27.

Kaplan, D. (1995). 'Statistical power in structural equation modeling', in R.H. Hoyle (ed.), *Structural Equation Modeling: Concepts, Issues, and Applications.* Thousand Oaks, CA: Sage.

Kido, A. (1986). 'Small group activity: A Japanese American comparison (in Japanese)', *Nihon Roumou Gakkai Nenpou.*

Kluckhohn, C. (1951). 'Values and value-orientations in the theory of actions: An exploration in definitions and classifications', in T. Parsons and E.A. Shils (eds), *Towards a General Theory of Action.* Cambridge, MA: Harvard University Press.

Kluckhohn, F.R. and Strodtbeck, F.L. (1961). *Variations in Value Orientations.* Evanston, IL: Row, Peterson & Co.

Knights, D. and McCabe, D. (1997). ' "How would you measure something like that?": Quality in a retail bank', *Journal of Management Studies*, 34(3): 371–88.

Knights, D. and McCabe, D. (1999). ' "Are there no limits to authority?": TQM and organizational power', *Organization Studies*, 20(2): 197–224.

Kroeber, A.L. (1917). 'The superorganic', *American Anthropologist*, 19(2): 163–213.

Kroeber, A.L. and Kluckhohn, C.K. (1952). *Culture: A Critical Review of Concepts and Definitions.* Cambridge, MA: Peabody Museum.

Laaksonen, O. (1988). *Management in China during and after Mao in Enterprises, Government, and Party.* Berlin: Walter de Gruyter.

Lascelles, D.B. and Dale, B.G. (1994). 'Difficulties and barriers to quality improvement', in B.G. Dale (ed.), *Managing Quality.* Second edition. Hertfordshire: Prentice Hall Europe.

Lau, S.K. and Kuan, H.C. (1988). *The Ethos of the Hong Kong Chinese.* Hong Kong: The Chinese University Press.

Lawrence, P. and Dyer, D. (1983). *Renewing American Industry.* New York: The Free Press.

Lee, C.C., Li, C.H. and Chan, K. (1996). 'Survey report: Republic of China', in T. Umeda (ed.), *TQM Practices in Asia-Pacific Firms.* Tokyo: Asian Productivity Organization.

Lee, R.P.L. (1985). 'Social stress and coping behavior in Hong Kong', in W.S. Tseng and D.Y.H. Wu (eds), *Chinese Culture and Mental Health.* New York: Academic Press.

Lee, T.Y. (1994). 'A Hong Kong experience of implementing ISO 9000: a research report on company certification (in Chinese)', *Hong Kong Economic Journal Monthly*, 213: 73–5.

Lee, T.Y. (1998). 'The development of ISO 9000 certification and the future of quality management: a survey of certified firms in Hong Kong', *International Journal of Quality and Reliability Management*, 15(2): 162–77.

Leonard, D. and McAdam, R. (2000). 'Grounded theory methodology and practitioner reflexivity in TQM research', *International Journal of Quality and Reliability Management*, 18(2): 180–94.

Leonard, F.S. and Sasser, W.E. (1982). 'The incline of quality', *Harvard Business Review*, 60(5): 163–71.

Leung, K. (1996). 'The role of beliefs in Chinese culture', in M.H. Bond (ed.), *The Handbook of Chinese Psychology.* New York: Oxford University Press.

Levitine, T. (1973). 'Values', in J.P. Robinson and P.R. Shaver (eds), *Measures of Social Psychological Attitudes.* Ann Arbor, MI: University of Michigan.

Lin, Y.T. (1935). *My Country and My People.* New York: Reynal and Hitchcock.

Lo, H.Y. (1998). 'A Chinese perspective on total quality management: The recapitulation of Confucian principles', *International Journal of Management*, 15(4): 508–15.

Lo, H.Y. (1999). 'The revealing of an oriental approach towards better quality: The intrinsic Confucianism of Chinese', in S.K.M. Ho (ed.), *TQM and Innovation: Proceedings of the Fourth International Conference on ISO 9000 and TQM*. Hong Kong: Hong Kong Baptist University.

Lu, M. (1983). *Confucianism: Its Relevance to Modern Society*. Singapore: Federal Publications.

Lundstrom, W.J. and Lamont, L.M. (1976). 'The development of a scale to measure customer discontent', *Journal of Marketing Research*, 8: 373–81.

Maccoby, M. (1994). 'Creating quality cultures in the East and West', *Research Technology Management*, 37(1): 57–9.

Malhotra, N.K. (1993). *Marketing Research: An Applied Orientation*. Englewood Cliffs, NJ: Prentice-Hall, Inc.

Manly, B.F.J. (1986). *Multivariate Statistics Methods: A Primer*. London: Chapman & Hall.

Mao, T.T. (1972). *Quotations from Chairman Mao Tsetung*. Peking: Foreign Language Press.

Martinsons, M.G. (1996). 'Cultural constraints on radical reengineering: Hammer and Lewin meet Confucius', *Journal of Applied Management Studies*, 5(1): 85–96.

Martinsons, M.G. and Hempel, P.S. (1998). 'Chinese business process reengineering', *International Journal of Information Management*, 18(6): 393–407.

Miyai, J. (1995). 'The redesign of Japanese management systems and practices', *APO Productivity Journal*, Summer, pp. 27–41.

Mizuno, S. (1979). *Managing for Quality Improvement: The Seven New QC Tools*. Cambridge, MA: Productivity Press.

Mizuno, S. (1988). *Company-Wide Total Quality Control*. Tokyo: Asian Productivity Organization.

Mondon, Y. (1982). *Toyota Production System*. New York: American Institute of Industrial Engineers.

Mueller, R.O. (1996). *Basic Principles of Structural Equation Modeling: An Introduction to LISREL and EQS*. New York: Springer Verlag.

Mulaik, S.A. (1987). 'Toward a conception of causality applicable to experimentation and causal modeling', *Child Development*, 58: 18–32.

Mulaik, S.A. and James, L.R. (1995). 'Objectivity and reasoning in science and structural equation modeling', in R.H. Hoyle (ed.), *Structural Equation Modeling: Concepts, Issues, and Applications*. Thousand Oaks, CA: Sage.

Muthén, B.O. (1992). 'Response to Freedman's critique of path analysis: Improve credibility by better methodological training', in J.P. Shaffer (ed.), *The Role of Models in Non-experimental Social Science: Two Debates*. Washington DC: American Educational Research Association.

Morris, C. and Jones, L.V. (1955). 'Value scales and dimensions', *Journal of Abnormal and Social Psychology*, 51: 523–35.

Napier, I. (1997). 'Australian culture and the acceptance of TQM', *APO Productivity Journal*, Winter, pp. 104–18.

Negandhi, A.R. (1986). 'Three decades of cross-cultural management research: Alice in Wonderland', in S. Clegg, D. Dunphy, and S.G. Redding (eds), *The Enterprise & Management in East Asia*. Hong Kong: University of Hong Kong.

Nita, M. (1978). 'JK activity in the iron and steel industry (in Japanese)', *Nihon Roudou Kyokai Zasshi*, 9.

Nunnally, J.C. (1978). *Psychometric Theory*. Second edition. New York: McGraw-Hill.

Onglatco, M.L.U. (1988). *Japanese Quality Control Circles: Features, Effects and Problems*. Tokyo: Asian Productivity Organization.

Parsons, T. (1951). *The Social System*. London: Routledge and Kegan Paul.

Parsons, T. (1956). 'Suggestions for a sociological approach to the theory of organizations-part I', *Administrative Science Quarterly*, June, pp. 63–85.

Peterson, M. and Cameron, K. (1995). *Total Quality Management in Higher Education: From Assessment to Improvement*. Ann Arbor, MI: University of Michigan.

Pike, K.L. (1954). *Language in Relation to a Unified Theory of the Structure of Human Behavior*. Glendale, CA: Summer Institute of Linguistics.

Powell, T.C. (1995). 'Total quality management as competitive advantage: A review and empirical study', *Strategic Management Journal*, 16(1): 15–37.

Prescott, B.D. (1995). *Creating a World Class Quality Organization: 10 Essentials for Business Success*. London: Kogan Page.

Price, F. (1984). *Right First Time*. Aldershot: Gower.

QC Circle Headquarters, Union of Japanese Scientists and Engineers (1980). *QC Circle Koryo: General Principles of the QC Circle*. Tokyo: QC Circle Headquarters, JUSE.

Recht, R. and Wilderom, C. (1998). 'Kaizen and culture: On the transferability of Japanese suggestion systems', *International Business Review*, 7: 7–22.

Redding, S.G. (1990). *The Spirit of Chinese Capitalism*. Berlin: Walter de Gruyter.

Redding, S.G. and Wong, G. (1986). 'The psychology of Chinese organizational behavior', in M.H. Bond (ed.), *The Psychology of the Chinese People*. New York: Oxford University Press.

Rokeach, M. (1973). *The Nature of Human Values*. New York: The Free Press.

Roney, J. (1997). 'Cultural implications of implementing TQM in Poland', *Journal of World Business*, 32(2): 152–69.

Ross, J.E. (1993). *Total Quality Management: Text, Cases, and Readings*. Boca Raton, FL: St. Lucie Press.

Rugman, A. (1981). *Inside the Multinationals*. New York: Columbia University Press.

Rungtusanatham, M., Forza, C., Filippini, R. and Anderson, J.A. (1998). 'A replication study of a theory of quality management underlying the Deming management method: Insights from an Italian context', *Journal of Operations Management*, 17: 77–95.

Saraph, J.V., Benson, P.G. and Schroeder, R.G. (1989). 'An instrument for measuring the critical factors of quality management', *Decision Sciences*, 20(4): 810–29.

Satorra, A. and Bentler, P.M. (1990). 'Model conditions for asymptotic robustness in the analysis of linear relations', *Computational Statistics and Data Analysis*, 10: 235–49.

Satorra, A. and Bentler, P.M. (1991). 'Goodness of fit test under IV estimation: Asymptotic robustness of a NT test statistic', in R. Gutierrez and M.J. Valderrama (eds), *Applied Stochastic Models and Data Analysis*. Singapore: World Scientific.

Schein, E.H. (1985). *Organizational Culture and Leadership*. San Francisco: Jossey Bass.

Schumacker, R.E. and Lomax, R.G. (1996). *A Beginner's Guide to Structural Equation Modeling.* Mahwah, NJ: Lawrence Earlbaum and Associates.

Schwartz, S.H. and Bilsky, W. (1987). 'Toward a universal psychological structure of human values', *Journal of Personality and Social Psychology*, 53(3): 550–62.

Schwartz, S.H. and Bilsky, W. (1990). 'Toward a universal psychological structure of human values: Extensions and cross-cultural replications', *Journal of Personality and Social Psychology*, 58(5): 878–91.

Shenkar, O. and von Glinow, M.A. (1994). 'Paradoxes of organizational theory and research: Using the case of China to illustrate national contingency', *Management Science*, 40(1): 56–71.

Shewhart, W.A. (1931). *Economic Control of Quality of Manufactured Products.* New York: Van Nostrand.

Shuster, D.H. (1990). *Teaming for Quality Improvement: A Process for Innovation and Consensus.* Englewood Cliffs, NJ: Prentice Hall.

Silin, R. (1976). *Leadership and Values.* Cambridge, MA: Harvard University Press.

Simon, A., Sohal, A. and Brown, A. (1994). 'Generative case study research in quality management part 1: Theoretical considerations', *International Journal of Quality and Reliability Management*, 13(1): 32–42.

Singh, P.N., Huang, S.C. and Thompson, G.G. (1962). 'A Comparative study of selected attitudes, values, and personality characteristics of America, Chinese, and Indian students', *Journal of Social Psychology*, 57: 123–32.

Smith, P.B. and Wang, Z.M. (1996). 'Chinese leadership and organizational structure', in M.H. Bond (ed.), *The Handbook of Chinese Psychology.* New York: Oxford University Press.

Smith, W.W. (1973). *Confucianism in Modern Japan: A Study of Conservatism in Japanese Intellectual History.* Tokyo: Hokuseido Press.

Sohal, A., Simon, A. and Lu, E. (1994). 'Generative case study research in quality management part 2: Practical examples', *International Journal of Quality and Reliability Management*, 13(2): 75–87.

Spencer, B.A. (1994). 'Models of organization and total quality management: A comparison and critical evaluation', *Academy of Management Review*, 19(3): 446–71.

Steingard, D.S. and Fitzgibbons, D.E. (1993). 'A postmodern deconstruction of total quality management', *Journal of Organizational Change Management*, 6(5): 27–42.

Strauss, A.L. and Corbin, J. (1990). *Basics of Qualitative Research.* Newbury Park, CA: Sage.

Sue, D.W. and Kirk, B.A. (1972). 'Psychological characteristics of Chinese-American students', *Journal of Counseling Psychology*, 19: 471–78.

Taguchi, G. (1986). *Introduction to Quality Engineering: Designing Quality into Processes.* Tokyo: Asian Productivity Organization.

Talley, D.J. (1991). *Total Quality Management: Performance and Cost Measures: The Strategy for Economic Survival.* Milwaukee, WI: ASQC Quality Press.

Taylor, F.W. (1911). *The Principles of Scientific Management.* New York: Harper & Brothers.

The Chinese Culture Connection (1987). 'Chinese values and the search for culture-free dimensions of culture', *Journal of Cross-Cultural Psychology*, 6(4): 143–64.

Triandis, H.C. and Marin, G. (1983). 'Etic plus emic versus pseudoetic: A test of a basic assumption of contemporary cross-cultural psychology', *Journal of Cross-Cultural Psychology*, 14(4): 489–500.

Triandis, H.C., McCusker, C., Betancourt, H., Iwao, S., Leung, K., Salazar, J.M., Setiadi, B., Sinha, J.B.P., Touzard, H. and Zaleski, Z. (1993). 'An etic-emic analysis of individualism and collectivism', *Journal of Cross-Cultural Psychology*, 24(3): 366–83.

Uemura, T. (1998). 'Japanization and late developer effects from cross-cultural X-efficiency', *Management Japan*, 31(1): 3–12.

Umeda, T. (1996). 'Integrated summary', in T. Umeda (ed.), *TQM Practices in Asia-Pacific Firms*. Tokyo: Asian Productivity Organization.

Wacker, J.G. (1986). 'How advanced is modern Chinese manufacturing management'? *International Journal of Operations and Production Management*, 7(3): 26–35.

Waldman, D.A. (1995). 'What is TQM research'? *Canadian Journal of Administrative Sciences*, 12(2): 91–94.

Wang, D.Y. (1992). 'The motivation of workers in the People's Republic of China: A comparison of work goals of employees in foreign-owned and state-owned enterprises', *Hong Kong Journal of Business Management*, 10: 19–36.

Weber, M. (1951). *The Religion of China*. New York: The Free Press.

West, S.G., Finch, J.F. and Curran, P.J. (1995). 'Structural equation models with non-normal variables', in R.H. Hoyle (ed.), *Structural Equation Modeling: Concepts, Issues, and Applications*. Thousand Oaks, CA: Sage.

Westphal, J.D., Gulati, R. and Shortell, S.M. (1997). 'Customization or conformity? An institutional and network perspective on the content and consequences of TQM adoption', *Administrative Science Quarterly*, 42: 366–94.

Whetten, D.A. (1989). 'What constitutes a theoretical contribution'? *Academy of Management Review*, 14(4): 490–94.

Wilkinson, A. and Willmott, H. (eds) (1995). *Making Quality Critical: New Perspectives on Organizational Change*. London: International Thomson Business Press.

Wilkinson, A., Redman, T. Snape, E. and Marchington, M. (1998). *Managing with TQM: Theory and Practice*. Hampshire: Palgrave.

Wilson, L.A. and Durant, R.F. (1994). 'Evaluating TQM: The case for a theory driven approach', *Public Administration Review*, 54(2): 137–46.

Wong S.L. (1991). 'Chinese entrepreneurs and business trust', in G. Hamilton (ed.), *Business Networks and Economic Development in East and Southeast Asia*. Hong Kong: University of Hong Kong.

Wood, J.M. and Tataryn, D.J. (1996). 'Effects of under and over extraction on principal axis factor analysis with varimax rotation', *Psychological Methods*, 1(4): 354–65.

Xu, Q. (1999). 'TQM as an arbitary sign for play: Discourse and transformation', *Organization Studies*, 20(4): 659–81.

Yang, K.S. (1970). 'Authoritarianism and evaluation of appropriateness of role behavior', *Journal of Social Psychology*, 80: 171–81.

Yang, K.S. (1972). 'Expressed values of Chinese college students (in Chinese)', in Y.Y. Li and K.S. Yang (eds), *Symposium on the Characteristics of the Chinese: An Interdisciplinary Approach*. Taipei: Institute of Ethnology, Academia Sinica.

Yang, K.S. (1986). 'Chinese personality and its change', in M.H. Bond (ed.), *The Psychology of the Chinese People*. New York: Oxford University Press.

Yang, K.S. (1996). 'Psychological transformation of the Chinese people as a result of societal modernization', in M.H. Bond (ed.), *The Handbook of Chinese Psychology*. New York: Oxford University Press.

Yang, K.S. and Ho, D.Y.F. (1988). 'The role of yuan in Chinese social life: A conceptual and empirical analysis', in A.C. Paranjpe, D.Y.F. Ho and R.W. Reiber (eds), *Asian Contributions to Psychology*. New York: Prager.

Yau, O.H.M. (1994). *Consumer Behavior in China: Customer Satisfaction and Cultural Values*. London: Routledge.

Yeung, C.L. and Chan, L.Y. (1999). 'Towards TQM for foreign manufacturing firms operating in mainland China', *International Journal of Quality and Reliability Management*, 16(8): 756–71.

Yin, R.K. (1989). *Case Study Research: Design and Methods*. Newbury Park, CA: Sage.

Yu, A.B. (1996). 'Ultimate life concerns, self, and Chinese achievement motivation', in M. Bond (ed.), *Handbook of Chinese Psychology*. New York: Oxford University Press.

Yu, J. and Cooper, H. (1983). 'A quantitative review of reassert design effects on response rates to questionnaires', *Journal of Marketing Research*, 20: 36–44.

Zhang, G.X. (1999). 'Beyond ISO 9000 certification: A China experience', *Managerial Auditing Journal*, 14(1): 75–8.

Zhao, X., Young, S.T. and Zhang, J. (1995). 'A survey of quality issues among Chinese executives and workers', *Production and Inventory Management Journal*, 36(1): 44–8.

Index

Note: Page numbers in **bold** refer to tables